✧ *Companions for the Journey* ✧

Praying with
Dorothy Day

✧ *Companions for the Journey* ✧

Praying with Dorothy Day

by
James Allaire
and
Rosemary Broughton

Saint Mary's Press
Christian Brothers Publications
Winona, Minnesota

✧ *To Barbara, Mary, Galen,* ✧
the Dan Corcoran Catholic Worker House,
and Catholic Workers everywhere.

✧ *To all the refugee families and friends of* ✧
Romero House in Toronto, especially Lorne Howcroft,
Mary Jo Leddy, and my fellow volunteers, Brian Halloran,
Peter Haeg, and Norbert Piché.

The publishing team for this book included Carl Koch, development editor; Barbara Augustyn Sirovatka, copy editor and typesetter; Lynn Dahdal, production editor; Elaine Kohner, illustrator; pre-press, printing, and binding by the graphics division of Saint Mary's Press.

The psalms on pages 61, 105, 109–110, 111, and 116 are from *Psalms Anew: In Inclusive Language,* compiled by Nancy Schreck and Maureen Leach (Winona, MN: Saint Mary's Press, 1986), pages 64, 197, 136–137, 88, and 88, respectively. Copyright © 1986 by Saint Mary's Press. All rights reserved.

The scriptural material found on pages 61, 72 (first excerpt), 79 (first and second excerpt), 97, and 115 is freely adapted and is not to be understood or used as an official translation of the Bible.

All other scriptural quotations used in this book are from the New Jerusalem Bible. Copyright © 1985 by Darton, Longman & Todd, Ltd., London; and Doubleday, a division of Bantam, Doubleday, Dell Publishing Group, New York. Used by permission of the publisher.

The acknowledgments continue on page 125.

Printed in the United States of America

Printing: 9 8 7 6 5 4 3

Year: 2003 02 01 00 1999 98

ISBN 0-88489-306-5

✧ **Contents** ✧

✧ Foreword ✧

Companions for the Journey

Just as food is required for human life, so are companions. Indeed, the word *companions* comes from two Latin words: *com*, meaning "with," and *panis*, meaning "bread." Companions nourish our heart, mind, soul, and body. They are also the people with whom we can celebrate the sharing of bread.

Perhaps the most touching stories in the Bible are about companionship: the Last Supper, the wedding feast at Cana, the sharing of the loaves and the fishes, and Jesus' breaking of bread with the disciples on the road to Emmaus. Each incident of companionship with Jesus revealed more about his mercy, love, wisdom, suffering, and hope. When Jesus went to pray in the Garden of Olives, he craved the companionship of the Apostles. They let him down. But God sent the Spirit to inflame the hearts of the Apostles, and they became faithful companions to Jesus and to each other.

Throughout history, other faithful companions have followed Jesus and the Apostles. These saints and mystics have also taken the journey from conversion, through suffering, to resurrection. Just as they were inspired by the holy people who went before them, so too may you take them as your companions as you walk on your spiritual journey.

The Companions for the Journey series is a response to the spiritual hunger of Christians. This series makes available the rich spiritual teachings of mystics and guides whose wisdom can help us on our pilgrimages. As you complete the last meditation in each volume, it is hoped that you will feel supported, challenged, and affirmed by a soul-companion on your spiritual journey.

The spiritual hunger that has emerged over the last twenty years is a great sign of renewal in Christian life. People fill retreat programs and workshops on topics in spirituality. The demand for spiritual directors exceeds the number available. Interest in the lives and writings of saints and mystics is increasing as people search for models of whole and holy Christian life.

Praying with Dorothy Day

Praying with Dorothy Day is more than just a book about her spirituality. This book seeks to engage you in praying in the way that Dorothy did about issues and themes that were central to her experience. Each meditation can enlighten your understanding of her spirituality and lead you to reflect on your own experience.

The goal of *Praying with Dorothy Day* is that you will discover Dorothy Day's rich spirituality and integrate her spirit and wisdom into your relationship with God, with your brothers and sisters, and with your own heart and mind.

Suggestions for Praying with Dorothy Day

Meet Dorothy Day, a fascinating companion for your pilgrimage, by reading the introduction to this book, which begins on page 13. It provides a brief biography of Dorothy and an outline of the major themes of her spirituality.

Once you meet Dorothy Day, you will be ready to pray with her and to encounter God, your sisters and brothers, and yourself in new and wonderful ways. To help your prayer, here are some suggestions that have been part of the tradition of Christian spirituality:

Create a sacred space. Jesus said, "'When you pray, go to your private room, shut yourself in, and so pray to your [God] who is in that secret place, and your [God] who sees all that is done in secret will reward you'" (Matthew 6:6). Solitary prayer is best done in a place where you can have privacy and silence, both of which can be luxuries in the life of busy people.

If privacy and silence are not possible, create a quiet, safe place within yourself, perhaps while riding to and from work, while sitting in line at the dentist's office, or while waiting for someone. Do the best you can, knowing that a loving God is present everywhere. Whether the meditations in this book are used for solitary prayer or with a group, try to create a prayerful mood with candles, meditative music, an open Bible, or a crucifix.

Open yourself to the power of prayer. Every human experience has a religious dimension. All of life is suffused with God's presence. So remind yourself that God is present as you begin your period of prayer. Do not worry about distractions. If something keeps intruding during your prayer, spend some time talking with God about it. Be flexible because God's Spirit blows where it will.

Prayer can open your mind and widen your vision. Be open to new ways of seeing God, people, and yourself. As you open yourself to the Spirit of God, different emotions are evoked, such as sadness from tender memories, or joy from a celebration recalled. Our emotions are messages from God that can tell us much about our spiritual quest. Also, prayer strengthens our will to act. Through prayer, God can touch our will and empower us to live according to what we know is true.

Finally, many of the meditations in this book will call you to employ your memories, your imagination, and the circumstances of your life as subjects for prayer. The great mystics and saints realized that they had to use all their resources to know God better. Indeed, God speaks to us continually and touches us constantly. We must learn to listen and feel with all the means that God has given us.

Come to prayer with an open mind, heart, and will.

Preview each meditation before beginning. After you have placed yourself in God's presence, spend a few moments previewing the readings and especially the reflection activities. Several reflection activities are given in each meditation because different styles of prayer appeal to different personalities or personal needs. **Note that each meditation has more**

reflection activities than can be done during one prayer period. Therefore, select only one or two reflection activities each time you use a meditation. Do not feel compelled to complete all the reflection activities.

Read meditatively. Each meditation offers you a story about Dorothy Day and a reading from her writings. Take your time reading. If a particular phrase touches you, stay with it. Relish its feelings, meanings, and concerns.

Use the reflections. Following the readings is a short reflection in commentary form, which is meant to give perspective to the readings. Then you are offered several ways of meditating on the readings and the theme of the prayer. You may be familiar with the different methods of meditating, but in case you are not, they are described briefly here:

✦ *Repeated short prayer or mantra:* One means of focusing your prayer is to use a *mantra,* or "prayer word." The mantra may be a single word or a short phrase taken from the readings or from the Scriptures. For example, the short prayer for meditation 6 in this book is "Jesus, pilgrim, you are my companion." Repeated slowly in harmony with your breathing, the mantra helps you center your heart and mind on one action or attribute of God.

✦ *Lectio divina:* This type of meditation is "divine studying," a concentrated reflection on the word of God or the wisdom of a spiritual writer. Most often in *lectio divina,* you will be invited to read one of the passages several times and then concentrate on one or two sentences, pondering their meaning for you and their effect on you. *Lectio divina* commonly ends with formulation of a resolution.

✦ *Guided meditation:* In this type of meditation, our imagination helps us consider alternative actions and likely consequences. Our imagination helps us experience new ways of seeing God, our neighbors, ourselves, and nature. When Jesus told his followers parables and stories, he engaged their imagination. In this book, you will be invited to follow guided meditations.

One way of doing a guided meditation is to read the scene or story several times, until you know the outline and can recall it when you enter into reflection. Or before your prayer time, you may wish to record the meditation on a tape recorder. If so, remember to allow pauses for reflection between phrases and to speak with a slow, peaceful pace and tone. Then, during prayer, when you have finished the readings and the reflection commentary, you can turn on your recording of the meditation and be led through it. If you find your own voice too distracting, ask a friend to make the tape for you.

✦ *Examen of consciousness:* The reflections often will ask you to examine how God has been speaking to you in your past and present experience—in other words, the reflections will ask you to examine your awareness of God's presence in your life.

✦ *Journal writing:* Writing is a process of discovery. If you write for any length of time, stating honestly what is on your mind and in your heart, you will unearth much about who you are, how you stand with your God, what deep longings reside in your soul, and more. In some reflections, you will be asked to write a dialog with Jesus or someone else. If you have never used writing as a means of meditation, try it. Reserve a special notebook for your journal writing. If desired, you can go back to your entries at a future time for an examen of consciousness.

✦ *Action:* Occasionally, a reflection will suggest singing a favorite hymn, going out for a walk, or undertaking some other physical activity. Actions can be meaningful forms of prayer.

Using the Meditations for Group Prayer

If you wish to use the meditations for community prayer, these suggestions may help:

✦ Read the theme to the group. Call the community into the presence of God, using the short opening prayer. Invite one or two participants to read one or both readings. If you use both readings, observe the pause between them.

✦ The reflection commentary may be used as a reading, or it can be deleted, depending on the needs and interests of the group.

✦ Select one of the reflection activities for your group. Allow sufficient time for your group to reflect, to recite a centering prayer or mantra, to accomplish a studying prayer *(lectio divina)*, or to finish an examen of consciousness. Depending on the group and the amount of available time, you may want to invite the participants to share their reflections, responses, or petitions with the group.

✦ Reading the passage from the Scriptures may serve as a summary of the meditation.

✦ If a formulated prayer or a psalm is given as a closing, it may be recited by the entire group. Or you may ask participants to offer their own prayers for the closing.

Now you are ready to begin praying with Dorothy Day, a faithful and caring companion on this stage of your spiritual journey. It is hoped that you will find her to be a true soul-companion.

CARL KOCH
Editor

Note: Dorothy Day did most of her writing before inclusive language came into general use. Because changing her words would be intrusive in the extreme, the passages have been unaltered. Given Dorothy's commitment to our common humanity and justice for all people, she would have approved of and employed inclusive language were she writing today. In writings near the end of her life, she did employ inclusive language.

✧ Introduction ✧

A Radical Lay Catholic

Dorothy Day's life and legacy is a radical movement, faithful to the Gospel and the church, immersed in the social issues of the day, with the aim of transforming both individuals and society. In an age marked by widespread violence, impersonal government, shallow interpersonal commitments, and a quest for self-fulfillment, Dorothy Day's spirit fosters nonviolence, personal responsibility of all people to the poorest ones among us, and fidelity to community and to God.

Dorothy Day's vision continues in the Catholic Worker Movement that she cofounded with Peter Maurin. Approximately 120 Catholic Worker communities serve in the United States, with new houses of hospitality opening every year. Dorothy left no rule or directions for the Catholic Worker communities. The rule she lived by and promoted is contained in the Gospels, most particularly in the Sermon on the Mount and in Matthew, chapter 25.

The vision of Dorothy Day lives on in *The Catholic Worker* newspaper that has been continually published since 1933. Dorothy was a journalist all her adult life, and she lived through and commented on the central events of the twentieth century: wars, economic depression, class struggle, the nuclear threat, and the civil rights movement. *The Catholic Worker* and her prodigious writings always focus the light of the Gospel on our conscience as we struggle with these issues. She wrote to comfort the afflicted and to afflict the comfortable.

These world issues and the suffering of humanity still challenge people of conscience to create a better world. Dorothy Day's response is essential Gospel: an old vision, so old it looks new. Her vision is anchored in the apostolic era and is essential for the atomic age. It challenges us to build community, grow in faith, and serve poor people. Her vision is a model of liberation for the United States.

Dorothy's Story

In her autobiography, *The Long Loneliness*, Dorothy divides her life into three parts. She describes her first twenty-five years as a time of "Searching" for a center of meaning and focus for her energies. During the middle period she calls "Natural Happiness," she lived in a common-law marriage, gave birth to a daughter, completed her conversion, embraced Catholicism, and turned her life in a new direction. The last and longest period, "Love Is the Measure," began when she met Peter Maurin and then cofounded the Catholic Worker Movement with him.

Childhood

Dorothy was born in Brooklyn, New York, on 8 November 1897 to Grace Satterlee Day, a New Yorker, and John Day, a Tennessean. Dorothy had two older brothers, Donald and Sam Houston. A sister, Della, and another brother, John, later joined the family.

When Dorothy was six years old, her father, a sports writer, took a job in California and moved the family to Oakland. He lost his job when the 1906 San Francisco earthquake destroyed the newspaper plant. Dorothy's memories of the quake and of her mother and the neighbors helping the homeless remained stamped in her mind. The family then moved to Chicago where they lived for the next ten years.

Dorothy grew up in a conventional middle-class home in the period before World War I. The Days valued reading, education, and writing. Her parents seemed to create a caring home. Nominally Protestant, the Days seldom attended church. Dorothy remembered being interested in religion and recalled reading the Bible, encountering neighbors praying, and at age eight being "disgustingly, proudly pious" (Dorothy Day, *The Long Loneliness: The Autobiography of Dorothy Day*, p. 20).

When Dorothy was ten, the rector of a nearby Episcopal church convinced Mrs. Day to enroll her sons in the choir. Dorothy started to attend church every Sunday. She loved the songs, especially the *Benedicite*, the *Te Deum*, and the psalms. When her family moved to the north side of Chicago, she studied the catechism so that she could be baptized and confirmed.

Dorothy read avidly. Her father insisted on keeping trashy dime novels out of the house. So even though she spent much of her time looking after John, the last of the Day children, Dorothy devoured the works of Hugo, Dickens, Stevenson, Cooper, Poe, and much of the socially conscious literature of Upton Sinclair and others. At sixteen, she won a scholarship and enrolled at the University of Illinois.

College: Searching in Earnest

During Dorothy's two years at the university, she established deep friendships, began her journalistic career, and developed a keen awareness of social conditions. While writing pieces for a local paper, she observed the disparity between the lives of rich and poor people. Subsequently, she joined the Socialist Party at the university. Even though the works of Dostoyevsky helped Dorothy retain a faith in God, she rejected organized religion because she perceived that it did nothing to alleviate the plight of desperate people.

At this time, Dorothy was poor herself, working odd jobs and living-in with families in exchange for doing laundry and child care. Regarding social problems, her critical sense sharpened:

> There was a great question in my mind. Why was so much done in remedying social evils instead of avoiding them in the first place? . . . Where were the saints to try to change the social order, not just to minister to the slaves but to do away with slavery? (*Long Loneliness*, p. 45)

The Searching Young Journalist

When Dorothy was eighteen, her family moved to New York. Dorothy followed and took her first job as a journalist with the *New York Call*, a socialist newspaper. Her reporter colleagues were socialists, communists, labor organizers for the American Federation of Labor and the Industrial Workers of the World (known as "Wobblies"), and various free thinkers and anarchists opposed to conscription and the entry of the United States into World War I.

Dorothy covered labor meetings and on one occasion traveled to Washington with a group of Columbia University students who opposed conscription. She reported on protests, the "bread riots" against the high cost of living, strikes, unemployment, and the many forms of human misery. The disparity between the classes and a critique of the present system formed the common thread in her reports.

Whether Dorothy personally endorsed the ideas she was writing about or whether they were more the product of her associations is not clear. Her accounts of this period highlight only the adventure of being close to people who were trying to change society. The street actions and the exciting debates of competing visions impressed Dorothy. Nevertheless, primarily she was a reporter, but one who advocated a point of view.

Dorothy's first jail experience occurred when she accompanied a group of women suffragists to the White House to protest the treatment of other suffragists in jail. While in jail, Dorothy joined a hunger strike and suffered great emotional desolation, a sense of the enormous evil that human beings can inflict on one another. She despaired at the efficacy of the protests and of her efforts: "What was right and wrong? What was good and evil? I lay there in utter confusion and misery" (*Long Loneliness*, p. 78).

Dorothy asked for a Bible and took great comfort from the psalms that expressed her own sorrow and hope. However, she did not want to go to God in this state of defeat. After the hunger strike succeeded, she again turned away from religion. Even so, being jailed was a significant experience for Dorothy, one that moved her from observation to participation, from being a passionate idealist to action. Her identification with the masses became real.

A Time of Drifting

During these years, Dorothy lead a bohemian lifestyle that she later described as dissolute, wasted, full of sensation and sensuality. The suicide of one of her circle overwhelmed Dorothy with the tragedy of life. She responded by signing on as a probationer at King's County Hospital in Brooklyn to study nursing. After a difficult year of demanding work, Dorothy abandoned her foray into nursing to again pursue writing. She saw clearly that this was her profession.

Dorothy had relationships with several men. After becoming pregnant, she had an abortion when she feared that the man she loved would leave her; the man deserted her anyway. She traveled to Europe, then drifted to Chicago, New Orleans, and briefly, California as a would-be screenwriter.

Even though the labor movement, socialist and communist ideas, and her own experiences of hardship had an indelible impact on Dorothy's commitment to social justice, this whole colorful period saw her drifting and searching. She had little to ground her spirituality, so at times she found herself dabbling in religious practices. She acquired a rosary in New Orleans and visited churches out of curiosity and in search of quiet and rest. She also observed and admired the religious faith of ethnic Catholics. Dorothy felt haunted by God and noted that even her former friends and comrades of the period remembered her talking about God.

The publication of her autobiographical novel, *The Eleventh Virgin*, closed her period of searching. She sold the screen rights for five thousand dollars. In 1924 a friend persuaded her to buy a beach house on Staten Island where she could settle down to study and write.

Natural Happiness

Life in the bungalow on Staten Island was a period of intense happiness. She entered into a common-law marriage with

Forster Batterham, a biologist whose political views Dorothy shared. Like her, he decried injustice and suffering. Life seemed idyllic: leisurely, simple, close to sea and sky, a cluster of friends close by. Forster helped Dorothy appreciate the beauty and wonders of the natural world around them.

This peaceful time for Dorothy also contained the seeds of change. Later she reflected:

> It was a peace, curiously enough, divided against itself. I was happy but my very happiness made me know that there was a greater happiness to be obtained from life than any I had ever known. I began to think, to weigh things, and it was at this time that I began consciously to pray more. (*Long Loneliness*, p. 116)

Dorothy prayed as she walked to get the mail, carried a rosary in her pocket, addressed the Blessed Virgin whose statue she had been given, was aware of God's mystery as she planted a seed, and recited the *Te Deum* as she worked about the house. She started regularly attending Sunday Mass. Dorothy's growing absorption in religion dismayed Forster. He saw religion as morbid escapism, and any talk about it immediately threw up a wall between them.

Tamar Teresa and Conversion

Dorothy had thought herself barren, but became pregnant. Years later she recalled, "I will never forget my blissful joy when I was first sure that I was pregnant" (*Long Loneliness*, p. 136). Forster opposed bringing children into the world, so this development only created more conflict between them.

During her pregnancy, Dorothy decided she would have her child baptized. Belonging to a faith, she thought, would give her child the order lacking in her own life. She prayed for the gift of faith for herself: "I was sure, yet not sure. I postponed the day of decision." She knew that if she became a Catholic, Forster would leave: "It was hard to contemplate giving up a mate in order that my child and I could become members of the Church. Forster wanted nothing to do with religion or with me if I embraced it. So I waited" (*Long Loneliness*, pp. 136–137).

Dorothy had been led to worship and prayer through the beauty of creation and the unutterable joy of Tamar Teresa's birth, but a detached and private faith did not satisfy her. She declared that her whole make-up as a radical led her to associate with others and be a part of the masses. For years Dorothy had seen the masses give their allegiance to the Catholic church in every city she lived in. For her, this ancient church was the church of the masses, so to it she gave her allegiance.

One day she saw a religious sister walking down the road and asked how she could have her daughter baptized. Sister Aloysia taught Dorothy her catechism, which she insisted be memorized, and brought her pious magazines to read. Dorothy found the piety tedious but decided to trust God.

After Tamar Teresa's baptism, the tension between Forster and Dorothy increased. Over the next months, he left her and the baby numerous times, but always returned. Dorothy hesitated to take the final step that she knew would irrevocably end her life with Forster. If she tried to talk about her faith, he grew silent. Dorothy loved him deeply and respected his anarchist and atheist views, but she could not envision becoming a Catholic and living with him. This tension dragged on into the next summer when Dorothy became ill and was diagnosed with a nervous condition.

During the winter of 1927, after an emotional explosion, Forster left again, Dorothy decided to end the torture for the two of them. When he tried to return, she would not let him in. The next day, she went to Sister Aloysia and was conditionally baptized, since she had already been baptized in the Episcopal church.

Dorothy continued writing and caring for Tamar. The Pathé movie studio in California offered her a contract to write for them. She did so for three months, but they actually gave her little work. She then went to Mexico for six months, partly to delay her return to New York since, "I hungered too much to return to Forster" (*Long Loneliness*, p. 158). After Tamar contracted malaria in Mexico, mother and daughter returned to New York City only to be greeted by the beginnings of the Great Depression.

In December 1932, the Catholic magazine *The Commonweal* commissioned Dorothy to write an article about a hunger march on Washington, D.C. The marchers, organized by the communists, sought social legislation to combat unemployment, establish pensions, and provide relief for mothers and children. As Dorothy stood on the curb watching, her heart swelled with pride and joy at the courage of the marchers, and she felt a bitterness that her conversion separated her from them:

> I could write, I could protest, to arouse the conscience, but where was the Catholic leadership in the gathering of bands of men and women together, for the actual works of mercy that the comrades had always made part of their technique in reaching the workers? (*Long Loneliness*, p. 165)

After she had written her story, Dorothy went to the national shrine of the Immaculate Conception in Washington. "There I offered up a special prayer, a prayer which came with tears and with anguish, that some way would open up for me to use what talents I possessed for my fellow workers, for the poor" (*Long Loneliness*, p. 166). When she returned to New York, she would find Peter Maurin waiting to meet her.

Love Is the Measure

Peter Maurin

Dorothy always insisted that Peter Maurin, not she, started the Catholic Worker Movement. She also credited him for completing her Catholic education.

The details of Peter Maurin's life are sketchy, but Dorothy recounts what he told her. He was born a French peasant and became a teacher with the De La Salle Christian Brothers in France. He emigrated to Canada, worked as an itinerant laborer in the United States, taught French in Chicago, then moved to New York. Constantly studying, Peter was charged with a vision to change the social order. Saint Francis of Assisi inspired him to live a life of voluntary poverty, and Peter was determined to popularize the social doctrines of the Catholic church.

Peter's vision was simple yet far-reaching. His program of action consisted of roundtable discussions for the clarification of thought, houses of hospitality where the works of mercy could be performed, and agronomic universities—a return to working the land, where workers could become scholars and scholars workers. He proposed to popularize this vision by publishing a newspaper for the people in the street.

When Peter met Dorothy, he introduced her to a whole new set of ideas and a historical vision of the Catholic church. Speaking in his thick French accent, he expounded on the prophets of Israel, the Fathers of the church, and the lives of the saints. Dorothy admired Peter both for the ideas he taught her and for his personal example of voluntary poverty and deep faith.

Peter also introduced her to his personalist philosophy and the French personalist writers, whose core belief is that all people share a common humanity: each of us becomes who we are meant to be by assuming personal responsibility for our brothers and sisters in need. "He stressed the need of building a new society within the shell of the old—that telling phrase from the preamble to the I.W.W. constitution, 'a society in which it is easier for people to be good,' he added with a touching simplicity, knowing that when people are good, they are happy" (*Long Loneliness*, p. 170). Peter stressed the need to perform the works of mercy at a personal sacrifice.

Peter, a visionary, hardly noticed what he ate or where he slept. Dorothy was more practical and action-oriented. Though Dorothy deeply respected Peter, he sometimes annoyed her with his zealous talking. Dorothy, who loved music, would scowl at Peter to be still while she tried to listen to a concert on the radio. Unfazed, Peter would find another listener and keep on talking. Dorothy once quipped, "When his mouth was full he would listen" (Dorothy Day, *Loaves and Fishes*, p. 20).

Nevertheless, through Peter's influence, Dorothy deepened her appreciation of Catholicism, especially of its social teachings. When Peter suggested starting a newspaper, something the journalist Dorothy could readily agree to, she had the vehicle for expressing the vision they shared.

The Catholic Worker Movement

On 1 May 1933, in the depths of the Great Depression, *The Catholic Worker* newspaper made its debut with a first issue of twenty-five hundred copies. Dorothy and a few others hawked the paper in Union Square for a penny a copy (still the price) to passersby. They called the paper *The "Catholic" Worker* because at the time many Catholics were poor. Peter and Dorothy wanted to influence Catholics, who were criticized for a lack of social and political morality. The paper was also for the worker in the broadest sense because it addressed, "those who worked with hand or brain, those who did physical, mental or spiritual work. But we thought primarily of the poor, the dispossessed, the exploited" (*Long Loneliness*, p. 204).

The Catholic Worker succeeded immediately, and circulation jumped to 100,000 by the end of the first year. Bundles of the paper found their way into parishes and schools around the country. Soon volunteers arrived to help with the work. Donations of food, clothing, and money came in to support them. A community grew quickly to feed the homeless and unemployed people who streamed to them, and the first house of hospitality opened.

What started as the effort of a newly converted Catholic laywoman and a French peasant on fire with a vision to transform society was becoming a movement. Intellectuals and ordinary laypeople alike responded wholeheartedly to this Catholic vision of social and personal transformation. It offered a more acceptable alternative at a time when many people thought that only the communists cared about the masses. Whether Dorothy sensed in 1933 that they had started a "permanent revolution," as she called it in *The Long Loneliness*, is not clear. But her prayer at the national shrine had been answered.

In the early days of the Catholic Worker Movement, Dorothy did what she did best. She wrote about the conditions of poor people and especially about the conditions of workers and the labor movement, then still struggling for recognition. She sought to synthesize Catholic social teaching in such a way that it would inspire volunteers, clergy, even bishops. Often she succeeded.

Some Catholic workers who came to New York went to other cities to form their own Catholic Worker houses. Within a few years thirty-three Catholic Worker houses and farms dotted the country. Although publishing the newspaper, offering hospitality at the houses, and assisting people through the works of mercy composed the chief work of the communities, Catholic Workers also joined street protests and labor pickets, helped with the housing and feeding of strikers, picketed the German consulate in 1935, and called for boycotts of stores where low wages or poor working conditions existed.

Inspired by Peter's vision, Catholic Worker farms strove to become agronomic universities. Oftentimes farms were donated to a worker community, but many of them failed for lack of resources or the necessary skills to live on the land. Dorothy acknowledged that they had to learn through grim experience. Some of the farms thrived and became rural havens for poor families, places of convalescence for the ill, getaways for slum children, and places where students discussed the green revolution that Peter envisioned.

Controversy

The Catholic Worker Movement soon met resistance. Dorothy's opposition to war and her pacifist stand during the Spanish Civil War divided supporters for the movement. Schools canceled their subscriptions to *The Catholic Worker*. Even so, Dorothy maintained her staunch pacifism and opposed in speech and writing all wars without exception, basing her position on Christ's command in the Sermon on the Mount to love our enemies.

In addition to writing of her challenging vision for every monthly edition of *The Catholic Worker,* Dorothy wrote articles for Catholic periodicals and two books. The personal testament of her search for God and eventual conversion became *From Union Square to Rome* (1938). *House of Hospitality* (1939) chronicled the early days of the Catholic Worker Movement.

The War Years

Resistance to Dorothy Day and the Catholic Worker Movement intensified as the nation went to war. For Dorothy it was a time of deepening, a necessary time of consolidation of her Catholic faith and of the ideas that fueled the Catholic Worker Movement. She was one of the few Catholic voices opposing World War II, as she had all previous wars, and not all those in the movement agreed with Dorothy's total pacifism. Many houses closed, some because the men who ran them were drafted. The bread lines shortened because of full employment for the war effort.

In 1943, Dorothy took a leave from the Catholic Worker Movement and spent some months on a solitary retreat near her daughter's boarding school. Tamar had grown up in the movement, and Dorothy's duties as a mother and the work at the Catholic Worker houses taxed them both. Now Dorothy wanted to be closer to her daughter as she matured.

Beginning around 1943, Peter Maurin's health started to deteriorate, and his mind began to fail him. When he realized the confused state of his thinking, he grew virtually silent, accepting his situation. Peter's decline was difficult for Dorothy to watch because he had played such a vital role in the formation of her vision.

Dorothy's spirituality up to this time had been fed by attending daily Mass, reading the lives of the saints and the New Testament, and performing the works of mercy. After attending conferences, days of recollection, and an intense rereat with Catholic Workers from the east coast and the Midwest, Dorothy very consciously began to focus on the Scripture message that we all share in the abundant love of God and that all of us are called to be saints. She concluded:

> This love, this foolishness of love, illustrated in the book of Osee in the Old Testament and in the story of the prodigal son in the New, this folly of the Cross, was the sum and substance of the retreat. . . . We must live this life now. . . . If we do not learn to enjoy God now we never will. (*Long Loneliness*, pp. 255–257)

During the last year of World War II, Dorothy and the Catholic Workers decided to turn one of the houses at the farm in Easton, Pennsylvania, into a retreat house. They began sponsoring retreats every few months that challenged participants to examine their conscience about the work they did, their material goods, and their attachments. Dorothy said that the style of the retreats "should be like a shock treatment," bringing new life by dying to the old self (*Long Loneliness*, p. 259). Eventually they sold the Easton farm and acquired Maryfarm in Newburgh, New York, where they continued the retreat work.

The retreats nourished Dorothy's spirit even though some members objected to their tone and emphasis. Coming after the first flush of success of the movement in the 1930s and during a time when Dorothy was a lone voice for pacifism and justice, the retreats helped Dorothy turn her prophetic witness toward the atomic age, civil rights, and later, to pacifism again when Vietnam dominated national life.

War Ends: The Struggle Continues

After World War II, only eleven Catholic Worker houses still carried on. So in 1946, Dorothy visited each one, trying to encourage the workers and reinvigorate the movement. A few commentators suggested at the time that the Catholic Worker Movement was a thing of the past, but Dorothy insisted that the need for servants of poor people was as relevant as ever. She was stung, however, by the criticism. The circulation of the newspaper was 190,000 in 1938, but largely because of its pacifist stand it now stood at 50,500.

In February of 1946, Dorothy began calling her column, "On Pilgrimage." In her own personal style, she chronicled the Catholic Worker Movement, commented on events, and talked about the books she was reading. She always looked at things from a spiritual point of view. Letters poured in, and Dorothy answered many of them, often using her travel time to catch up on correspondence.

With the war behind the country, Dorothy and *The Catholic Worker* continued to critique industrial capitalism and especially the popular notion that machines liberated the worker. Dorothy argued that most factory work debased work and the worker. She favored decentralization and local or regional solutions to problems. Dorothy did not reject all machine technology; indeed, she relished driving cars. However, she felt that work should be creative and humanizing rather than mechanical and dehumanizing. When critics labeled her an anarchist or socialist, she responded by calling herself a Christian personalist.

Then Peter Maurin died on 15 May 1949. He had spent the last years of his life at the Catholic Worker farm in Newburgh, New York. To Dorothy, Peter Maurin was her teacher and the Saint Francis of our times. She continued to eulogize him in her writings for the rest of her life. Peter's death was a deep, personal loss.

Carrying on the Worker movement, fostering the retreat movement, and caring for her family filled Dorothy's days. Tamar had married and started her own family. In 1948 Dorothy spent an extended time with Tamar and her husband, David Hennessy, at their farm in West Virginia as Tamar awaited the birth of her fourth child. The country air and her playful grandchildren delighted Dorothy. She wrote about this in her book *On Pilgrimage*.

For Dorothy, these few years again proved a time of deepening, of acquiring a more profound sense of her vocation and mission. Her writing for *The Catholic Worker* and other periodicals continued. Dorothy's daily life consisted of practicing her spiritual devotions (Mass, parts of the Divine Office, meditation and reading, and other prayers), getting the paper out, traveling and speaking frequently, and managing the New York Worker houses. This rhythm provided a faithful regularity to her life.

The 1950s

The Catholic Worker had been arguing against the A-bomb since Hiroshima, and the subject was about to become a personal cause for Dorothy Day. In 1955, Dorothy, a group of Catholic Workers, and others led protests against New York City's civil defense law. They declared that the air-raid drills deceived people into believing that they could actually survive a nuclear attack. So instead of taking shelter as the sirens sounded to begin the drill, Dorothy and the protesters merely sat on park benches. During the six years these drills occurred, they repeated their protests. Dorothy was jailed three times, once for a month. From this experience, Dorothy penned several strong articles about life in prison.

The Catholic Worker was now an established and distinctive voice within Catholic journalism. During the McCarthy-era of anti-Communism, some charged that *The Catholic Worker* supported communism. But anyone who studied the paper knew that "the personalist position of Peter Maurin and Dorothy Day . . . was the most fundamental and clear-cut anticommunist idea and program that had been defined by an

American Catholic voice" (William D. Miller, *Dorothy Day: A Biography*, p. 434).

Dorothy's autobiography, *The Long Loneliness*, published in 1952, made her life and vision available to a wide readership, especially since it was broadly reviewed. Some years later, Dorothy wrote *Therese*, her biography of Thérèse of Lisieux.

The 1960s

Turbulence marked the 1960s. Characteristically, Dorothy and the Catholic Worker Movement responded. Since its beginnings in 1933, *The Catholic Worker* had carried articles about racism, the exploitation of black labor, and justice for minorities. When the civil rights movement gained momentum in the 1960s, other articles added a clear voice for equality and justice among people of all races. When Martin Luther King was killed, Dorothy wrote:

> Martin Luther King died daily, as St. Paul said. He faced death daily and said a number of times that he knew he would be killed for the faith that was in him. The faith that men could live together as brothers. The faith in the Gospel teaching of nonviolence. The faith that man is capable of change, of growth, of growing in love. (Dorothy Day, *The Catholic Worker*, April 1968)

During the Vietnam war, Dorothy actively supported conscientious objectors and advocated only nonviolent protest. Dorothy was among the small group of people that started American PAX, later to become Pax Christi. The name change delighted Dorothy because she believed that Christ stood at the heart of true peace.

Dorothy admired the enthusiasm, energy, and outrage at injustice of the many young people who joined the Catholic Worker Movement during this period. However, elements of their lifestyle troubled her, perhaps because they seemed to mirror the mistakes of her own youthful searching.

In 1963 Dorothy traveled to the Vatican in support of Pope John XXIII's encyclical *Pacem in Terris* and to ask for a more radical condemnation of the instruments of modern warfare.

Later that year, she spoke at an English Catholic Conference on voluntary poverty, draft resistance, civil rights, and pacifism. Also in 1963, her book *Loaves and Fishes* was published. It tells the story of the Catholic Worker Movement and some of the people and events that were significant in its development.

The Catholic Worker Movement acquired a farm at Tivoli, New York, and it became the best embodiment of all their efforts toward a retreat and conference center. Beginning in July 1964 and continuing for the next decade, the PAX Tivoli Conference was held there. Lively thought, prayer, enjoyment of the arts, and fellowship all intermingled.

In September 1965, Dorothy was part of a PAX delegation to the last session of the Vatican Council II. The delegation hoped to influence the bishops to issue a strong peace statement that included support of conscientious objection, the validity of Gospel nonviolence, and a ban on nuclear weapons. Dorothy and nineteen other women fasted for ten days as a penitential offering for the success of the council. Eventually the council published "The Church in the Modern World," which included a condemnation of indiscriminate warfare, supported conscientious objection, linked arms expenditures with the unmet needs of poor people, and pointed to Gospel nonviolence as a conscionable position for Catholics. Dorothy's personal account of this decade appeared in a collection of her reflections entitled *On Pilgrimage: The Sixties* (1972).

Her Last Years

In 1970, as Dorothy was speaking in Detroit, a nurse in the audience pointed out that Dorothy needed medical attention. At age seventy-three, Dorothy suffered from shortness of breath that came from water in her lungs, hardening of the arteries, and an enlarged heart. Medicine somewhat relieved the condition, but her heart was failing.

Although Dorothy tired easily, she accompanied her close friend Eileen Egan on a world tour and then on a journey to Russia in the next year. In India, she met Mother Teresa and spoke to the novice sisters about going to prison for the sake of the Gospels. Dorothy was widely known by this time, and many groups honored her for the goodness of her life and her work on behalf of peace and justice. But the traveling, and even the honors, took a further toll on her body.

In 1973, at age seventy-six, Dorothy joined Cesar Chavez and the United Farm Workers in California's San Joaquin Valley for a nonviolent demonstration against the Teamsters Union (IBT). She was arrested with other protesters and jailed for ten days. This was Dorothy's last imprisonment.

Although Dorothy needed long periods of rest, she continued to struggle with the rapid pace of change and the erosion of traditional practice in the church and among the followers of the movement. She chided herself as an old fogy, but lamented that so many young workers seemed to turn away from sustaining religious practices. Perhaps reliving her own youthful searching piqued her sadness. Her faith had challenged and comforted her, but the exodus of so many priests and religious distressed her.

Her speech before the Eucharistic Congress in Philadelphia on 6 August 1976 was her last. Dorothy departed from her prepared text and spoke from the heart about her love of God, about the necessity of taking that love into all creation, and about the church that gave her the life of the Spirit. True to form, she reminded the assembly that the day was Hiroshima Day and that acts of destruction directly opposed God who "gave us life, and the Eucharist to sustain our life" (Miller, *Dorothy Day*, p. 513).

Shortly after this talk, Dorothy suffered a heart attack. Virtually confined to bed, she wrote a few letters when her strength permitted. Her daughter and grandchildren made frequent visits. She died in the early evening of 29 November 1980 with Tamar at her side.

So many people came to her funeral at Nativity Church in New York City that many had to stand outside on the sidewalk. During her life, Dorothy Day refused to let people "dismiss her as a saint" (Eileen Egan, *Dorothy Day and the Permanent Revolution*, p. 19). At her death, many of her admirers used the word openly. A "permanent revolution" had been initiated by Dorothy's leadership, grounded in the Sermon on the Mount for which she had "prayed, spoken, written, fasted, protested, suffered humiliation and gone to prison" (p. 25).

Dorothy's Spirituality

Two broad spiritual streams came together in Dorothy Day's character, and each stream contributed to her spirituality. As an American born into a Protestant family that valued education and literacy, she was a pragmatist, a worker, and a woman of action. After her conversion, these traits united with the traditions of Roman Catholicism: the teachings of the papal social encyclicals, the sacramental and liturgical life and sense of sacramentality, and the devotion to and imitation of the saints and mystics. Dorothy's love of the Scriptures came from her Protestant roots and predated the widespread use of the Bible by lay Catholics.

Characteristics

Dorothy Day's spirituality is marked by these characteristics:

Love of Scripture: Throughout her life, Dorothy received comfort and inspiration from the Bible, especially the Psalms, the Pauline writings, and the Gospels. They were part of her daily meditation, and scripture verses and images spontaneously wove themselves into her writings. The example and teachings of Christ were at the heart of her spirituality.

Solidarity with the Poor: In the Catholic Worker community, Dorothy shared her daily energies with and on behalf of poor people. Her writings, direct practice of the works of mercy, and her own voluntary poverty bound her to poor, homeless, sick, and desperate people.

Personalism: Dorothy loved doing works of mercy because they allowed her to take direct and immediate action for her brothers and sisters in Christ and against the ills of society that robbed them of their life, freedom, and dignity. Her engagement with other people flowed from her wholeness as a person; her heart and mind were cultivated through her reading, reflection, conversations, writing, and worship. She wanted the fullness of life for herself and every person.

Prophetic Witness: By her public words and work, Dorothy sought to imitate Christ's witness against injustice, even when such witness seemed folly. Like Christ, she was critical of the powers and structures of injustice and endured ridicule and opposition for her witness.

Peacemaking: A steadfast pacifist, Dorothy opposed all wars and the use of force and violence to solve human problems. She practiced and promoted human dignity with the spiritual weapons of prayer, fasting, almsgiving, civil disobedience, and works of amendment. Like Jesus, the woman at the well, and Saint Paul, she took her message to the people in the streets.

A Sacramental Sense: Dorothy looked to sacramental celebrations, especially the Eucharist, for daily spiritual sustenance, and she saw the world, its people and all of nature, to be full of God's grandeur and love as well.

Gratitude: In good times and in bad, Dorothy had a keen sense of appreciation and learned to trust in the providence of God. Dorothy regularly expressed gratitude not only to God but to those around her and to *The Catholic Worker*'s readers.

Dorothy for Today

Although Dorothy spurned the suggestion that she was a saint, she took seriously the importance of becoming one; saintly people could heal the ills of this world. God created the Mystical Body of Christ for holiness, wholeness, and sanctity. Jesus took on humanity to show people how to be godly through acting justly, loving tenderly, and walking humbly. The Holy Spirit continually invites all Christians to holiness.

Dorothy Day provides a contemporary model of the qualities of holiness: solidarity with and service to God's poor, promoting and being willing to suffer for justice, acting in charity, living in community, integrating faith and action through prayer, sacred ritual, and meditation. Dorothy Day may not always be a comfortable companion on the spiritual journey, but she will certainly be a wise, caring, and challenging one.

✧ Meditation 1 ✧

Turning to God

Theme: Conversion—turning to God—is an act of faith and a gift of love. Through all of our experiences, God invites us into intimate relationship.

Opening prayer: O God, in the strength of my joy in your goodness, turn my whole heart to you and your will.

About Dorothy

The birth of her child, Tamar Teresa, turned Dorothy to God in joy. Even though the birth effectively ended her long relationship with Forster Batterham, being mother to Tamar, living at her Staten Island beach home, and absorbing the sounds and rhythms of the wind, sand, sea, and surf made life joyful and satisfying. About this time of conversion, she wrote, "What a driving power joy is! When I was unhappy and repentant in the past I turned to God, but it was my joy at having given birth to a child that made me do something definite" (*Long Loneliness*, p. 141).

Later as she retraced her encounters with God and the long journey to her conversion, Dorothy recounted awakening to God's presence while holding a Bible found in the attic of her childhood home in Berkeley. She remembered early church experiences, such as going to Sunday services and singing hymns. She recalled coming upon her friend's mother, Mrs. Barrett, on her knees praying as she herself was racing through the Barrett home to find her childhood friend Katherine. Seeing Mrs. Barrett's devotion stopped Dorothy in awe and filled her with affection.

While in her twenties, Dorothy was arrested and jailed while marching for women's suffrage. Hoping to receive the privileges due political prisoners, the women marchers fasted. Dorothy experienced acute physical and mental anguish while fasting. She picked up the book of Psalms and found in them the expression of her own heartfelt cries and needs. Once released from jail and back in her old milieu, she discounted this praying with a sense of guilt and distaste. She saw turning to prayer as a weakness and as a display of her vulnerability. Sometime later though, Dorothy admitted that in praying the Psalms, she had been touched by the reality of God's strength and had joined those people who had been transformed by the prayers throughout the ages.

All these encounters with the sacred converged when Dorothy gave birth to Tamar Teresa. Six years later, after a demonstration in Washington, D.C., that she was covering as a journalist for *The Commonweal*, Dorothy wended her way to the national shrine of the Immaculate Conception. There she prayed that some way would open up for her to use what talents she possessed for her fellow workers and for poor people.

Soon after, Peter Maurin entered her life. Together they founded the Catholic Worker Movement, and Dorothy's turn to God took a more definite shape. She focused her faith, her story, and her talents in the loving service of God's people.

Pause: Ponder this question: As my story has unfolded, how has God's loving presence touched my heart?

Dorothy's Words

"Thou shalt love the Lord thy God with thy whole heart and with thy whole soul and with thy whole mind." This is the first Commandment.

The problem is, how to love God? We are only too conscious of the hardness of our hearts, and in spite of all that religious writers tell us about *feeling* not being necessary, we do want to feel and so know that we love God.

"Thou wouldst not seek Him if thou hadst not already found Him," Pascal says, and it is true too that you love God if you want to love Him. One of the disconcerting facts about the spiritual life is that God takes you at your word. Sooner or later one is given a chance to prove his love. The very word "diligo," the Latin word used for "love," means "I prefer." It was all very well to love God in His works, in the beauty of His creation which was crowned for me by the birth of my child. Forster had made the physical world come alive for me and had awakened in my heart a flood of gratitude. The final object of this love and gratitude was God. No human creature could receive or contain so vast a flood of love and joy as I often felt after the birth of my child. With this came the need to worship, to adore. I had heard many say that they wanted to worship God in their own way and did not need a Church in which to praise Him, nor a body of people with whom to associate themselves. But I did not agree to this. My very experience as a radical, my whole make-up, led me to want to associate myself with others, with the masses, in loving and praising God. (*Long Loneliness*, pp. 138–139)

Reflection

Conversion can be hidden or manifest. Some people wake up one day or catch themselves spontaneously performing a great act of generosity and realize "I am in love" or "I really care about this person, and I want what is good for them." The same movement holds true for people who in their affections or acts discover that they love God. In many cases they do not know the day or the hour that they started deliberately to love God.

Other people are able to track more consciously the movements of grace in their lives, its discomforts and its allures. Dorothy Day seems to be one of these people. She articulates the moment of her saying yes to the grace of God. She underscores both the deep satisfaction of faith and the excruciating choices that she needed to make in the face of it.

God has time, and God takes time. In telling the story of her life, Dorothy Day gives us access to the events, feelings, and experiences that drew her to a committed act of faith in God. She also explains the manner of life and mission that flowed from her change of heart and from her continued reading and reflection on the Gospels. Her final embrace of God's love ended her rootlessness and drifting.

✧ Conversions are often recognized as culminating experiences that mark a fresh beginning. Spend time reflecting on a conversion experience in your life, a time when you took a turn toward fuller love of God and your neighbor. Recall the time; if possible, go to the place. Relive the thoughts, feelings, crisis issues, leaps of faith, and pertinent persons all present in this experience. Pray for the gift of renewing the vitality and commitment of this experience.

✧ After a conversion, phases and experiences are recognized as paths along the way. If you don't have a journal, consider starting one. In your journal, write about the phases in your life when you sensed the presence of God calling you to something more whole, something beyond the scope of the life you were leading. Imagine that you are sharing your story with Dorothy as friend to friend. Compose a closing prayer, recognizing the providence of God guiding you.

✧ Conversion has consequences. It calls us to change our thoughts, attitudes, and behaviors. Reflect on changes that you have made in the past because of your faith. Ask for light and strength for changes that may be asked of you now. In a letter to God, speak of your thoughts and feelings, fears and desires about your ongoing conversion.

✧ Conversions take place in environments. Write in your journal about a natural environment that seems to be conducive to you in experiencing the call of God and in living out that call according to your talents. Then write about the social milieu that seems to be the appropriate one for your call and mission.

✧ Are there any surprises for you after this reflection? Are there any changes called for in "how to love God?" Ask God for any help that you need. Jot down any calls to action that emerge during this prayer.

God's Word

A lawyer stood up and, to test [Jesus], asked, "Master, what must I do to inherit eternal life?" He said to him, "What is written in the Law? What is your reading of it?" He replied, "You must love . . . God with all your heart, with all your soul, with all your strength, and with all your mind, and your neighbour as yourself." Jesus said to him, "You have answered right, do this and life is yours." (Luke 10:25–28)

Closing prayer: Come, O Holy Spirit, fill the hearts of your faithful and enkindle in them the fire of your love.

✧ **Meditation 2** ✧

Belonging to the Mystical Body

Theme: As Dorothy's relationship with Christ expanded, she reached a profound understanding that belonging to the Mystical Body of Christ unites us to all people and calls us to embrace everyone as our neighbor.

Opening prayer: Open my eyes, O Christ, to see you in my brothers and sisters.

About Dorothy

Dorothy's devotion to the Mystical Body of Christ allowed her to integrate her faith with her sense of social solidarity. Even as a young woman, she felt profound emotions about and a strong bond with two immigrant workers, Nicola Sacco and Bartolomeo Vanzetti, who were arrested on charges of theft and the murders of a shoe-factory paymaster and guard in Massachusetts. Doubt of their guilt led to widespread support and worldwide protests. When she heard about their impending execution, Dorothy wrote:

> While I enjoyed the fresh breeze, the feel of salt water against the flesh, the keen delight of living, the knowledge that these men were soon to pass from this physical

earth, were soon to become dust, without consciousness, struck me like a physical blow. They were here now; in a few days they would be no more. (*Long Loneliness*, pp. 145–146)

Dorothy also experienced a rush of sympathy for the family and friends of the shoeworker and fish peddler who, many thought, were unfairly tried because they were anarchists:

They had become figures beloved by the workers. Their letters, the warm moving story of their lives, had been told. Everyone knew Dante, Sacco's young son. Everyone suffered with the young wife who clung with bitter passion to her husband. And Vanzetti with his large view, his sense of peace at his fate, was even closer to us all. (P. 146)

The International Workers of the World (IWW) had taken up the cause of the two men. Dorothy knew well the union's slogan: "An injury to one is an injury to all." She wrote:

The day they died, the papers had headlines as large as those which proclaimed the outbreak of war. All the nation mourned. All the nation, I mean, that is made up of the poor, the worker, the trade unionist—those who felt most keenly the sense of solidarity—that very sense of solidarity which made me gradually understand the doctrine of the Mystical Body of Christ whereby we are the members one of another. (P. 147)

Dorothy's solidarity with other people gave power to her writing and to her actions. One of the editors at *The Catholic Worker* who lived with Dorothy recalled how she wanted to publish stories of how people helped each other:

We should be talking about what was building up the Mystical Body, showing what people were doing, how they were throwing in their lot. So people all across the world could say, "Gee, look at these people! They just opened up their house to people, or they decided to create a small school for mothers who didn't have any place to leave their children when they were going to work." Often [Dorothy] would prefer to start the paper with articles like that and then move to the more theoretical things. She loved to have letter columns because, once again, there was that human voice coming in. (Rosalie R. Troester, comp. and ed., *Voices from the Catholic Worker*, p. 62)

Dorothy loved to quote from letters she had received so that personal stories with a human voice could be told.

Pause: What feelings and sense of purpose does belonging to the Mystical Body of Christ awaken in you?

Dorothy's Words

If Mr. Gottlieb around the corner in his little grocery store should ask us what we mean by the Mystical Body of Christ, what shall we tell him? And if a member of the Order of Seventy-six, or a Communist, a striker or scab, a Jew, a Gentile, or a Negro, or a Japanese?

How could we tell it any better than in Christ's own words? "I am the vine; you are the branches."

Or in the words of St. Paul: "We are members, one of another. . . ."

An understanding of the dogma of the Mystical Body is perhaps the greatest need of the present time. It is a further explanation of the Incarnation. . . .

Christ is the head and we are the members. And the illnesses of injustice, hate, disunion, race hatred, prejudice, class war, selfishness, greed, nationalism, and war weaken this Mystical Body, just as prayer and sacrifices of countless of the faithful strengthen it.

St. Augustine says that we are all members or potential members of the Mystical Body of Christ.

Therefore all men are our neighbors and Christ told us we should love our neighbors, whether they be friend or enemy.

St. Augustine warns us never to judge another because we do not know what he may be in the future. (Dorothy Day, "The Mystical Body of Christ," *The Catholic Worker*, October 1939)

Reflection

Dorothy found great consolation and challenge in the Mystical Body of Christ. She spoke of her communion not only with social martyrs and ordinary people on the street but also with bigots and racists. In her writings, she wanted to announce the good things people were doing to build up not only human society but the Mystical Body of Christ.

In belonging to the Mystical Body, Dorothy enjoyed the ethnic diversity around her: Lithuanian, Italian, Irish, French, African, and German. Her belief in the Mystical Body of Christ compelled her to fight divisions, ills, and hatreds with weapons of the spirit: prayer, penance, and active love. It called her to great compassion and tact in dealing with the suffering, weak, neglected, and ignored members of society. Christ is the vine; we are the branches.

✧ In harmony with your breathing, meditate on this phrase: "We are all members, one of another."

✧ Go to a quiet place with your journal and respond in writing to the following: If someone from your own family asked you the meaning of the Mystical Body, what would you answer? If someone from your own social group asked you the same question, what would you answer? Someone from a cultural or ethnic group not your own? Take time to pray about your responses.

✧ Dorothy kept alert to the national and international happenings of the day and let her heart be moved. She suffered with those who suffered and rejoiced with those who rejoiced. Read the paper or listen to the news today. Take time to let yourself resonate with the cause and events of others in their sufferings and in their joys.

✧ Find a way to experience other cultures or ethnic groups, such as going to an ethnic fair or a different neighborhood. Use all your senses to become more attentive to this new ethnic world. An alternative experience could be watching a video or reading a novel set in another culture. Spend time at the end of the day praying for the people whose gifts, cultural history, or stories of courage most impressed you.

✧ Our prejudices need to be examined and challenged from time to time. Reflect on any person or group for whom you harbor some prejudice. Examine the roots of this prejudice. Pray for the gift of a changed heart. Choose one action to practice for ten days that is in accord with a changed heart.

Then reflect on a person or a group that acts prejudicially toward you. Pray for the gift of an understanding heart. Choose one action to practice for ten days that is in accord with an understanding heart.

✧ "If one part is hurt, all the parts share its pain." Reflect on an instance where this sense of solidarity was true for you. "And if one part is honored, all the parts share its joy." Reflect on an event in which this was true for you.

God's Word

For as with the human body which is a unity although it has many parts—all the parts of the body, though many, still making up one single body—so it is with Christ. We were baptized into one body in a single Spirit, Jews as well as Greeks, slaves as well as free . . . , and we were all given the same Spirit to drink. (12:12–13)
. . . God has composed the body so that greater dignity is given to the parts which were without it, and so that there may not be disagreements inside the body but each part may be equally concerned for all the others. If one part is hurt, all the parts share its pain. And if one part is honoured, all the parts share its joy. (1 Corinthians 12:24–26)

Closing prayer: Open my eyes, O Christ, that I may see you in my sisters and brothers of every nation, color, and creed. Open my ears that I may hear you in their words. Open my hands that I may be generous. Open my heart that your love may unite us.

Extending Hospitality

Theme: Hospitality is the basic Christian act of sharing what we have with others in need. It was an essential expression of Dorothy's spirituality.

Opening prayer: God, create a generous heart within me. Open my eyes to see your need in the needs of other people.

About Dorothy

One cold February in the early years of the Catholic Worker Movement, when everyone's energy was low, two women staying at Maryhouse were squabbling over keeping the window open in their room. One liked plenty of fresh air at night; the other wanted only snug warmth since she tramped the streets during the day looking for work. Another fuss broke out over cleaning the bathtub, and some of the guests insisted that a sign saying "WASH OUT THE TUB" be hung in the bathroom.

Dorothy and the editors were trying to get out *The Catholic Worker* newspaper, but tasks of hospitality kept intruding. The women at Maryhouse needed to discuss their problems and sometimes came into the office to talk, or they lingered at the table after lunch for conversation and companionship. Meals for ten women and the staff had to be made. Every day many visitors stopped in, and donated clothes had to be sorted and distributed.

Sometimes the guests volunteered to help in the common kitchen, and that lightened the load. One pregnant, unmarried, and penniless woman was more concerned that Peter's effort to start a Worker's School would go well than about her own lack of food, clothing, and shelter.

Somehow the people of Maryhouse cared for twenty-five women that February. Someone occupied every bed, but no one had to be turned away. Dorothy remarked, "Always, when a new one came in, another, providentially, was leaving for a job" (Dorothy Day, *House of Hospitality*, p. 44). Dorothy overheard one of the newspaper's editors remark, "Even if only one person were served and helped by the House of Hospitality, *The Catholic Worker* would be repaid and could feel that its labors were not in vain" (p. 43).

Pause: How do you offer hospitality to other people?

Dorothy's Words

It is no use saying that we are born two thousand years too late to give room to Christ. Nor will those who live at the end of the world have been born too late. Christ is always with us, always asking for room in our hearts.

But now it is with the voice of our contemporaries that He speaks, with the eyes of store clerks, factory workers, and children that he gazes; with the hands of office workers, slum dwellers, and suburban housewives that He gives. It is with the feet of soldiers and tramps that He walks, and with the heart of anyone in need that He longs for shelter. And giving shelter or food to anyone who asks for it, or needs it, is giving it to Christ.

. . . All that the friends of Christ did for Him in his lifetime, we can do. Peter's mother-in-law hastened to cook a meal for Him, and if anything in the Gospels can be inferred, it surely is that she gave the very best she had, with no thought of extravagance. Matthew made a feast for Him, inviting the whole town, so that the house was in an uproar of enjoyment, and the strait-laced Pharisees—the good people—were scandalized.

The people of Samaria, despised and isolated, were overjoyed to give Him hospitality, and for days He walked and ate and slept among them. And the loveliest of all relationships in Christ's life, after His relationship with His Mother, is His friendship with Martha, Mary, and Lazarus and the continual hospitality He found with them. It is a staggering thought that there were once two sisters and a brother whom Jesus looked on almost as His family and where He found a second home. . . .

If we hadn't got Christ's own words for it, it would seem raving lunacy to believe that if I offer a bed and food and hospitality to some man or woman or child, I am replaying the part of Lazarus or Martha or Mary, and that my guest is Christ. There is nothing to show it, perhaps. There are no halos already glowing round their heads—at least none that human eyes can see. . . .

We can do it too, exactly as they did. We are not born too late. We do it by seeing Christ and serving Christ in friends and strangers, in everyone we come in contact with.

. . . He said that a glass of water given to a beggar was given to Him. He made heaven hinge on the way we act toward Him in His disguise of commonplace, frail, ordinary humanity. . . .

And to those who say, aghast, that they never had a chance to do such a thing, that they lived two thousand years too late, He will say again what they had a chance of knowing all their lives, that if these things were done for the very least of His brethren they were done to Him. (Dorothy Day, "A Room for Christ," *The Catholic Worker*, December 1945)

Reflection

Offering hospitality can be full of surprises. Perhaps we have entertained angels—messengers of God—as the author of Hebrews 13:2 suggests. Dorothy learned from Peter Maurin how hospices for poor or wayfaring people were common in the Middle Ages. Peter quoted Saint Jerome, who said in the fourth century that every house should have a "Christ room" for those in need. Peter shared a vision of hospitality with Dorothy where love of neighbor was a matter of personal responsibility. Except in times of great crises such as floods, hurricanes, earthquakes, and drought, it was not a function of the state.

Hospitality consists of both attitude and concrete acts. As an attitude, hospitality implies a basic openness to others, a willingness to admit that what I have is yours too in your moment of need. Hospitality is a willingness to open one's space and time to another.

As a concrete act, hospitality means welcoming people to our table to share food and conversation, providing them clean clothing, offering a bath and a bed: domestic, basic human needs. Hospitality lets us feel we are at home.

Hospitality takes time, and we often feel driven by a sense of urgency and lack of time. Dorothy certainly had lots to do, but she had a wonderful sense of time as it relates to hospitality:

> If we are rushed for time, sow time and we will reap time. Go to church and spend a quiet hour in prayer. You will have more time than ever and your work will get done. Sow time with the poor. Sit and listen to them, give them your time lavishly. You will reap time a hundredfold. (*Long Loneliness*, p. 252)

Dorothy reminds us that we always have the opportunity to serve Christ disguised in friends, strangers, and everyone we come in contact with.

✧ Read Dorothy's Words again slowly, picking a scene from the Gospels she describes and elaborating it further in your imagination. Place yourself there, feel the joy, partake of the generosity, sense the graciousness, participate in the hospitality. Recall times you have been a guest of others, perhaps in another country or with people of another culture. Thank God for such hospitality and, if possible, thank those who showed hospitality to you.

✧ Dorothy recalls Jesus visiting Martha and Mary and how each had a style of her own: one bustled around, and the other was content to sit in silence. Reflect on your style of hospitality. Are you more a Martha, more a Mary, or some of both? Are you satisfied with your style? Would you prefer to be more Martha-like or Mary-like? Imagine yourself in each role. Imagine how you would offer hospitality to Jesus if he came to stay with you for the weekend. What might you do differently when you next offer hospitality?

✧ Consider the characteristics of hospitality Dorothy gleans from the gospel stories. For Dorothy, hospitality is first a privilege, and it should be generous and even extravagant, always personal and concrete. She wrote: "What a delightful thing it is to be boldly profligate, to ignore the price of coffee and go on serving the long line of destitute men who come to us, good coffee and the finest of bread" (*Long Loneliness*, p. 235). Allow your next act of hospitality to be enlivened with these qualities.

✧ What opportunities for hospitality to the poor are there today in your community? List possibilities. If you have a spare or guest room, discern how you might use it as a "Christ room." Imagine how you and some friends or your faith community might start a House of Hospitality in the Catholic Worker tradition.

✧ Use the words "they all ate as much as they wanted" from God's Word as a mantra, weighing each word as you softly repeat the phrase.

God's Word

When evening came, the disciples went to [Jesus] and said, "This is a lonely place, and time has slipped by; so send the people away, and they can go to the villages to buy themselves some food." Jesus replied, "There is no need for them to go: give them something to eat yourselves." But they answered, "All we have with us is five loaves and two fish." So he said, "Bring them here to me." He gave orders that the people were to sit down on the grass; then he took the five loaves and the two fish, raised his eyes to heaven and said the blessing. And breaking the loaves he handed them to his disciples, who gave them to the crowds. They all ate as much as they wanted. (Matthew 14:15–20)

Closing prayer: I am grateful, gracious God, for your gift of love and for all the good things present in my life. Increase in me a willingness to share what I have with the stranger that I welcome in your name. When I next offer hospitality, may it be an occasion for enjoying simple, nourishing food, and a time of unhurried conversation and sweet refreshment for weary souls.

The Spiritual Works of Mercy

Theme: Dorothy may be best known for feeding and clothing poor people, but she believed strongly in performing the spiritual works of mercy as well. She realized that they open the way for God's love and truth to act through us to inspire, encourage, and comfort others.

Opening prayer: O God, you shower me with kindness and mercy. May I be as generous in doing the spiritual works of mercy.

About Dorothy

The spiritual works of mercy were Dorothy's guidelines for the principal activities of her life. These works are to admonish the sinner, to instruct the ignorant, to counsel the doubtful, to comfort the sorrowful, to bear wrongs patiently, to forgive all injuries, and to pray for the living and the dead.

Peter and Dorothy decided that with his vision and her journalistic skill, they would publish an eight-page monthly paper for the people on the street. They hoped *The Catholic Worker* would instruct the ignorant, counsel the doubtful, and admonish the sinner.

Over time, Dorothy found herself writing books as well as articles, speaking to groups around the country, sponsoring Catholic Worker retreats, and picketing in public demonstrations. These works too spoke to the human spirit on its way to God.

Dorothy also prayed for the living and the dead. Jim Forest says of her:

> When I think of Dorothy, I think of her first and foremost as a woman at prayer. Dorothy was a praying person. If she was at the farm in Tivoli, there was a fairly good chance you'd find her in the chapel. Either there or at the table drinking coffee with visitors.
>
> If she was in the chapel, she'd be by herself, even if other people were there. Those old knees and those thick, dark stockings and those bulky shoes. She'd be there for a long time. I'm sure it wasn't that comfortable for her to be on her knees at that point. I can remember—nosy, snooping-around person that I was and still am—going up to look into her missal or Bible or whatever she had left on the pew, looking through and seeing all these lists of people she was praying for. In that unmistakable italic-like handwriting.
>
> Dorothy realized there was no time with God, only eternity. In fact, one of the most important parts of her intercession was praying for people who had committed suicide. She had a great deal of sympathy for them. . . . You couldn't reverse the fact that they were dead. You couldn't change history in that way, but you could perhaps change something about that person's death or something that happened in that person's thoughts. I'm not sure what she was doing, but she knew that she could pray for them and that God's eternity is different than time. (Troester, *Voices*, p. 79)

Pause: Ask yourself: Have I been called to perform a particular spiritual work of mercy today?

Dorothy's Words

We have always acknowledged the primacy of the spiritual, and to have undertaken a life of silence, manual labor and prayer might have been the better way. But I do not know. God gave us our temperaments, and in spite of my pacifism, it is natural for me to stand my ground, to continue in what actually amounts to a class war, using such weapons as the works of mercy for immediate means to show our love and to alleviate suffering.

And the weapons of journalism! My whole life had been in journalism and I saw the world in terms of class conflict. I did not look upon class war as something to be stirred up, as the Marxist did. I did not want to increase what was already there but to mitigate it. When we were invited to help during a strike, we went to perform the works of mercy, which include not only feeding the hungry, visiting the imprisoned, but enlightening the ignorant and rebuking the unjust. We were ready to "endure wrongs patiently" for ourselves (this is another of the spiritual works of mercy) but we were not going to be meek for others, enduring *their* wrongs patiently. . . .

Peter used to say when we covered strikes and joined picket lines, "Strikes don't strike me." Yet he took the occasion to come out on the picket line to distribute leaflets upon which some single point was made. "To change the hearts and minds of men," he said. "To give them vision—the vision of a society where it is easier for men to be good." (*Long Loneliness*, p. 181)

Reflection

The Catholic Worker Movement began with the newspaper, the houses of hospitality, roundtable discussions for clarification of thought, and with attempts at agronomic universities. The movement intended to afflict the comfortable and comfort the afflicted. It would go to the person on the street with the news that the Catholic church cared about them and had an agenda for social reform that had been articulated in the papal encyclicals.

Dorothy was aware that God gave us our temperaments and that her temperament allowed her to publicly confront injustice in her writings. As a member of a democratic and pluralistic society, Dorothy knew that this kind of prophetic witness involved risk. She upbraided herself sometimes as being too full of pride when she caught herself using strident language. Often before she wrote or spoke, she would spend time in church, asking God for the grace to find the right words, words at once faithful to the Gospel and full of love.

As you consider the spiritual works of mercy, first accept your basic temperament as a gift from God. Then consider applications that are both public and personal.

✧ Admonish the sinner: Take time to think about how Peter Maurin and Dorothy Day practiced this spiritual work of mercy. Think of what it means for you and how you have practiced or have resisted practicing it. Petition God for what you need. If possible, share in a roundtable discussion or talk with a trusted friend about how this can and should be practiced today.

✧ Instruct the ignorant: Parents, coaches, educators, supervisors, and artists practice this work of mercy constantly. Think of the situations in which you give other people guidance in life or the confidence that comes from knowledge. Pray for those you instruct, and ask for wisdom. Thank God for those who have instructed you.

✧ Counsel the doubtful: Pray for all professionals who give counsel to others that they may be guided by the truth and the desire for the well-being of others. As friends we are often called upon to listen to each other's worries, fears, and joys. Whenever we share our experience in confidence with others, we are performing this work of mercy. Give thanks for your counselors, and pray for those to whom you give counsel.

✧ Comfort the sorrowful: Take time today to listen to those you know are grieving or carrying heavy burdens, maybe even yourself. Ask them what they would like for you to do. Be with those sorrowing the best way you know how.

✧ Bear wrongs patiently: Meditate slowly on each word: bear, wrongs, patiently. Think of present situations in your life in which you are called to do this, either in your roles in the community as worker or citizen or in your small circle of friends and family. Pray for the gifts of hope and perseverance, and for the wisdom and courage to confront wrongs when that is possible.

✧ Forgive all injuries: Place yourself consciously in the presence of God. Speak to God of what has most injured you recently. Use a psalm or just cry out to vent your inmost feelings to God. Then ask for the balm of the Spirit for your injury, for the situation in which it occurred, and for those who have perpetrated the injury. Spend time reflecting on the call to a concrete action of reconciliation.

✧ Pray for the living and the dead: Take time early in the day to write the names of five living persons who need your prayers in a special way. As you write their names, visualize them, hear their voices, and petition God for what they most need. Take time late in the day to write the names of five deceased persons who come to mind. Recall some event from their life that has made them significant to you. Ask God to hold them in an eternal, loving embrace.

God's Word

Love is always patient and kind; love is never jealous; love is not boastful or conceited, it is never rude and never seeks its own advantage, it does not take offense or store up grievances. Love does not rejoice at wrongdoing, but finds its joy in the truth. It is always ready to make allowances, to trust, to hope and to endure whatever comes.

Love never comes to an end. . . .

As it is, these remain: faith, hope and love, the three of them; and the greatest of them is love. (1 Corinthians 13:4–8,13)

Closing prayer: Kindly God, be merciful to me. I stand in need of your guidance in using the gifts that you have given me. Send your Holy Spirit, and the gifts of the Spirit, to heal the human family and to guide our life together.

The Corporal Works of Mercy

Theme: Dorothy believed that doing the corporal works of mercy manifests our fidelity to the Gospel's call to help whoever lacks the basic necessities of life: nourishment, security, and compassion. Her legacy of practicing the corporal works of mercy continues at the Catholic Worker houses of hospitality.

Opening prayer: Merciful God, you feed the hungry and rescue those in trouble. Empower me to be the hands and heart of your mercy in my world.

About Dorothy

All her life, Dorothy believed that God intended that all people should have what they need to maintain the gift of life. She recalled thinking at fifteen:

> We did not need to have quite so much destitution and misery as I saw all around and read of in the daily press.
> . . .
>   . . . I wanted life and I wanted the abundant life. I wanted it for others too. I did not want just the few, the missionary-minded people like the Salvation Army, to be

kind to the poor, as the poor. I wanted everyone to be kind. I wanted every home to be open to the lame, the halt and the blind, the way it had been after the San Francisco earthquake. Only then did people really live, really love their brothers. In such love was the abundant life and I did not have the slightest idea how to find it. (*Long Loneliness*, pp. 38–39)

Through the catechism and meditation on chapter 25 of Matthew's Gospel, Dorothy learned that in Christian tradition, feeding the hungry, giving drink to the thirsty, clothing the naked, ransoming the captives, sheltering the homeless, visiting the sick and imprisoned, and burying the dead were called the corporal works of mercy. Even before her conversion, she had practiced many of these works of mercy.

Her conversion and subsequent sad experiences drew her more deeply to merciful actions:

As volunteers came to join the small group putting out "The Catholic Worker," a communal kitchen grew. Hungry people came for coffee, bread and soup. Some of them asked for shelter, but there was simply no room in the East Fifteenth Street tenement. Dorothy related [how] one day two women who had shared a meal told her they were homeless. They walked out into the street. One came back to tell Dorothy that her companion had thrown herself under a subway train. With her only five dollars in her hand, Dorothy walked down Fifteenth Street to a tenement with a vacant apartment. She rented it with the five dollar deposit and it provided shelter for six homeless women. This was the first House of Hospitality. (Egan, *Permanent Revolution*, p. 5)

The works of mercy became the abiding norm of the Catholic Worker Movement. Triggered by tragedy or moved by enthusiasm, Dorothy acted on the words she read in the Gospel. She took personal responsibility for the good of her sisters and brothers.

Pause: How do the corporal works of mercy give life to your spirituality?

Dorothy's Words

The Corporal Works are to feed the hungry, to give drink to the thirsty, to clothe the naked, to ransom the captive, to harbor the harborless, to visit the sick, and to bury the dead.

When Peter Maurin talked about the necessity of practicing the Works of Mercy, he meant all of them. He envisioned Houses of Hospitality in poor parishes in every city of the country, where these precepts of Our Lord could be put into effect. He pointed out that we have turned to state responsibility through home relief, social legislation, and social security, that we no longer practice personal responsibility, but are repeating the words of the first murderer, "Am I my brother's keeper?"

The Works of Mercy are a wonderful stimulus to our growth in faith as well as love. Our faith is taxed to the utmost and so grows through this strain put upon it. It is pruned again and again, and springs up bearing much fruit. For anyone starting to live literally the words of the Fathers of the Church—"The bread you retain belongs to the hungry, the dress you lock up is the property of the naked"; "What is superfluous for one's need is to be regarded as plunder if one retains it for one's self"—there is always a trial ahead. "Our faith, more precious than gold, must be tried as though by fire. . . ."

It is by the Works of Mercy that we shall be judged. (Dorothy Day, "The Scandal of the Works of Mercy," *The Commonweal*, 4 November 1949)

Reflection

The corporal works of mercy are undertaken to insure the basic necessities of life: shelter, nourishment, and compassion in times of suffering and sorrow.

The word *mercy*, as we commonly use it today, contains connotations of tenderness, forbearance, and pity. The biblical sense of mercy is more closely related to words that express

God's love such as compassion, mother's love, grace, security, and goodness. God's love can be trusted. It is stable, a rock. The works of mercy are acts of love.

Dorothy invites us to take Jesus' words in Matthew 25 seriously and to act on them. The corporal works of mercy are named by Jesus as the criteria—the bottom line—for entrance into the Kingdom of God. By our mercy, we also help bring about the Reign of God here on earth. Taking personal responsibility in some way to meet the basic needs of life for poor people is nonnegotiable in the Gospel.

Acting mercifully has its own rewards. The results of our efforts, which may strain us, will strengthen our faith and our ability to love.

✧ Read the list of the seven corporal works of mercy and pause after each one. Consider how you personally perform each work of mercy. For each work of mercy, complete the sentence. For example, "I feed the hungry when . . .", substituting the name of each in the sentence. Consider poor people close at hand in your family, among your neighbors, or the people you work with, as well as needy people in distant lands.

✧ Examine your conscience regarding the corporal works of mercy. First, read the God's Word section of this meditation or the full scripture in Matthew 25:31–46. Then imagine yourself at the judgment scene, standing before the Christ. Jesus asks you these questions, and you respond to each one:
+ "Did you feed the hungry?"
+ "Did you visit the sick or imprisoned?"
+ "Did you give refreshing drink to the thirsty?"
+ "Did you clothe the naked?"
+ "Did you make room for strangers?"

For all the times when you acted mercifully, give thanks to God. For the merciless times, pray the Jesus Prayer that Dorothy was fond of: "Jesus Christ, son of the living God, have mercy on me, a sinner."

✧ Recall a time in your life when you were without food, clothing, or shelter, or when you were sick and no one visited you. Enter into the feelings of that situation. If it is still true for you, pray to God for deliverance. If it is a past experience, thank God for the reversal. If you cannot remember a time of desperate need, spend a generous portion of time in thanksgiving at your local church or by ministering at a food bank, homeless shelter, or in some other work of mercy. Thank God for all the people who have provided for you during your life.

God's Word

When Jesus the Christ comes in glory, all the people of the earth will be gathered before him. He will divide them just like a shepherd sorts the sheep from the goats. The sheep will go to the right and the goats to the left. Then Christ will tell those at his right hand: "Come, take your rightful place in God's house. After all, when I was hungry, you fed me. When I burned with thirst, you gave me water. When I was a homeless stranger, you gave me shelter and welcome. Without a shirt on my back, you clothed me. In jail and sick, you kept me company."

The righteous will ask Christ. "But when did we do all these works of mercy for you?" And Christ will reply: "When you acted mercifully to any poor person, you acted mercifully to me." (Adapted from Matthew 25:31–40)

Closing prayer:

Happy those who aid the poor and the lowly.
God will help them when they are in trouble.
Yahweh will protect and preserve them,
will make them happy in the land.

(Psalm 41:1–2)

✧ **Meditation 6** ✧

On Pilgrimage

Theme: Dorothy saw clearly that life is a long journey to God. While on this pilgrimage, we are given many opportunities to proclaim the Good News.

Opening prayer: Living God, you travel faithfully with me on my pilgrimage. Help me to sense your presence and know that I am not alone.

About Dorothy

Dorothy traveled extensively around the country and to other nations. In her travels, Dorothy visited the Catholic Worker houses, lectured at colleges and universities, and talked to women's clubs in parish churches. She met with people actively engaged in the struggle for justice for workers, pacifism, and the plight of the homeless. She traveled by car, train, and very often by bus. Traveling by bus in particular helped her stay close to ordinary people. While riding, she read, reflected, and often answered correspondence.

Dorothy entitled her column in *The Catholic Worker*, "On Pilgrimage." The happenings on her journeys frequently provided material for her column. Traveling served as a metaphor for living, and her column often pondered how Christ accompanies us on the journey and challenges us to love.

On one bus journey, a cheerful driver was informing the passengers about the building of the Holland tunnel as they passed through it on leaving New York. This prompted Dorothy to reflect on the construction of the Golden Gate bridge in San Francisco:

> How many lives were lost on these roads, these bridges and tunnels which common men built and dug! You cannot travel by bus without having these ideas impressed upon you, up through the all but impenetrable canyons where power lines have been carried, pipe has been laid, roads have been built, if not stone by stone as in Roman times then actually foot by foot of slow and daily progress from one end of the vast country to the other. It makes you more patient with the slow work you are doing, the small job, the making of meals, the giving out of clothes, the building of that bridge of love from man to man, the creation of a sense of community, fellowship. (Dorothy Day, "Traveling by Bus," *The Commonweal*, 10 March 1950, p. 577)

Pause: Ask yourself: What pilgrimage am I on now?

Dorothy's Words

A few weeks ago, I again made a solitary pilgrimage to Auriesville, on my way back from speaking engagements at Rochester and Geneseo, New York. . . .

I remained for a time in front of the statue of St. Isaac Jogues, thinking of that former pilgrimage so long ago. And suddenly it came to me: I had been going around the country, and yes, to Mexico, Italy, and England too, speaking for many, many years now, telling the story of the Catholic Worker movement and its perennial philosophy of work and poverty, as the basis of peace and as an expression of the love of God and love of brother. For thirty-four years I have spent months of every year in travelling and speaking, and I never left our house of hospitality in New York, or one of our farms, without a wrench, without a sickness at having to go. And yet I was convinced that this was my vocation. Years ago, Father McSorley, of the Paulists, who was my first spiritual advisor, had told me to go where I was asked. I enjoyed all the trips, the meetings with all our groups and speaking at all our houses over the years, and I learned much from the encounters I had with other speakers and other groups, priests and people. I never came back without feeling enriched, and convinced too, that we were on the right path. (Dorothy Day, *On Pilgrimage: The Sixties*, pp. 281–282)

Reflection

Seeing our life as a pilgrimage suggests that each step on our destination is a holy place. Like Dorothy, we leave home. We learn as we go; we face situations as they come; we are purposeful, yet mobile. We notice surroundings. We listen to stories and recount them. On some pilgrimages we are seeking; on other pilgrimages, we are sent. Each step of the way, God moves with us, if we only acknowledge God's presence. Each experience is a chance for wisdom and an invitation to love.

The temptation to cease traveling, to hold fast to what we have and who we are, can be powerful. However, refusing to budge from the safe and known stifles our relationship with God and our ability to love more expansively. Pilgrimage spirituality challenges us to reach out to other people and, when we realize that our own resources are inadequate for the next mountain, to reach out for the always faithful hand of God.

✧ Dorothy liked to quote Catherine of Siena, "All the way to heaven is heaven, because He had said, 'I am the Way'" (*Long Loneliness*, p. 247). Meditate on this sentence, word by word.

✧ Go on a pilgrimage to a chosen destination: a church, a friend's home, a soup kitchen, a hospice, a prison, or a place of natural beauty. Prepare a prayer of petition or thanksgiving to be used at your arrival. Recall that Jesus is at your side; ask for any special grace that you need while you are journeying.

✧ Dorothy was told that she should go where she was asked. What would that advice mean for you?

✧ What pilgrimage are you on now? Use pen and paper, paints, chalk, water colors, or crayon to depict your pilgrimage artistically. Remember that knowing you are on pilgrimage means your artwork does not have to be perfect. Once you finish, ponder your picture. What do you feel? Are there any surprises?

✧ Take time today to carefully listen to others. Ask them what they hope for, where they are going, what they really want. Pray with them about their future; ask for what they need in the present moment.

✧ Do you ever feel tempted to stay put, to refuse to move forward, or to put a halt to accepting new challenges to relationships and service? What are the sources of these temptations? Talk with Jesus, the wanderer who never had a place to rest his head, about the desire to cease the pilgrimage. Ask for the grace you need to stay the course.

✧ In the God's Word section following, Jesus walks with the disciples on their pilgrimage to Emmaus. Write your own dialog with the questions you would like to ask Jesus. Remember, he accompanies you all the time.

✧ Today as you drive to work, or move about your home or office, offer this prayer: "Jesus, pilgrim, you are my companion."

God's Word

Two of them were on their way to a village called Emmaus, seven miles from Jerusalem, and they were talking together about all that had happened. And it happened that as they were talking together and discussing it, Jesus himself came up and walked by their side; but their eyes were prevented from recognizing him. He said to them,

"What are all these things that you are discussing as you walk along?" (13–17)

When they drew near to the village to which they were going, he made as if to go on; but they pressed him to stay with them saying, "It is nearly evening, and the day is almost over." So he went in to stay with them. Now while he was with them at table, he took the bread and said the blessing; then he broke it and handed it to them. And their eyes were opened and they recognized him; but he had vanished from their sight. Then they said to each other, "Did not our hearts burn within us as he talked to us on the road and explained the scriptures to us?" (Luke 24:28–35)

Closing prayer: O God of life, be with me on my pilgrimage to you. Help me to stay the course, choose life and movement forward, and be generous in the use of the gifts you gave me. Be my life's companion.

Work

Theme: In all our work, whether manual, mental, or spiritual, we are called to be collaborators with God, to spread the
lavish, divine love to the earth and to all people. Through this
understanding, Dorothy deeply respected workers and stood
in solidarity for their dignity and rights.

Opening prayer: Creator God, let all the work of my
hands, head, and heart praise you. May my work reflect your
love of me in the talents that I have.

About Dorothy

Dorothy worked principally as a journalist and author. Her
writing helped to support her, Tamar, and the Catholic Worker Movement. Through writing she also expressed her faith.

When she finished writing the book *On Pilgrimage*, she
added this at the end:

> It is the work of a journalist who writes because it is her
> talent, it has been her means of livelihood and it is sent
> out with the hopes that it will *sell*, so that the printing bill
> will be paid, and enough left over to bring out another
> book next year. . . . It is written most personally because
> I am a woman who can write no other way. If it is preach-
> ing and didactic in parts it is because I am preaching and

teaching and encouraging myself on this narrow road we are treading. (Pp. 174–175)

Over her writing career, Dorothy published eight books, more than three hundred articles in Catholic and other periodicals, and hundreds more signed and unsigned contributions to *The Catholic Worker* newspaper.

Throughout her life, Dorothy wrote a great deal about work and workers. During her early apprenticeship as a journalist with the radical press, she covered efforts to organize workers. When *The Catholic Worker* appeared in 1933, unemployment was widespread. The paper gave generous space to labor issues before legislation existed regarding union rights, unemployment benefits, and workplace conditions. During and after World War II when work was abundant, Dorothy wrote about the machine age and the dehumanizing conditions of the assembly line. In the 1970s, she would again write about the plight of migrant workers and in support of Cesar Chavez and the farmworkers.

Many of Dorothy's views on work came through Peter's emphasis on a philosophy of work. For Peter, human dignity required that persons be able to support themselves and their family through meaningful work. Dorothy repeated Peter's motto, "work, not wages" throughout her writings. "A philosophy of work is essential if we would be whole men, holy men, healthy men, joyous men" ("On Pilgrimage," *The Catholic Worker*, May 1948). Dorothy and Peter were also influenced by the Benedictine tradition of *ora et labora* (prayer and work), where work is in balance with worship and leisure, leading to an integrated life.

Pause: Is your work helping you be holy, whole, and healthy?

Dorothy's Words

Man is a creature of body and soul, and he must work to live, he must work to be co-creator with God, taking raw materials and producing for human needs. He becomes

God-like, he is divinized not only by the Sacrament but by his work, in which he imitates his Creator, in which he is truly "putting on Christ and putting off the old man." (*The Catholic Worker,* November 1962)

Christ lived among men. The great mystery of the Incarnation, which meant that God became man that man might become God, was a joy that made us want to kiss the earth in worship, because His feet once trod the same earth. It was a mystery that we as Catholics accepted, but there were also the facts of Christ's life, that He was born in a stable, that He did not come to be a temporal King, that he worked with His hands, spent the first years of His life in exile, and the rest of His early manhood in a crude carpenter shop in Nazareth. He fulfilled His religious duties in the synagogue and the temple. He trod the roads in His public life and the first men He called were fishermen, small owners of boats and nets. He was familiar with the migrant worker and the proletariat, and some of His parables dealt with them. He spoke of the living wage, not equal pay for equal work, in the parable of those who came at the first and the eleventh hour. (*Long Loneliness,* pp. 204–205)

If our jobs do not contribute to the common good, we pray God for the grace to give them up. Have they to do with shelter, food, clothing? Have they to do with the Works of Mercy? Everyone should be able to place his job in the category of the Works of Mercy.
. . . Whatever has contributed to the misery and degradation of the poor may be considered a bad job, and not to be worked at. (*The Catholic Worker,* December 1948)

Reflection

The selections in Dorothy's Words focus on her deepest convictions about work. Through our work we exercise our essential dignity as persons created in God's image. Work is a means of providing us with what we need to live, but it is also a way to holiness. During his life, Jesus worked as a carpenter, associated with poor workers, and defended laborers. Our approach to work and our jobs, then, needs to be evaluated according to the principles of human dignity and justice that Jesus exemplified for us.

In Dorothy's lifetime, the world of work underwent a profound transformation. From a still largely agrarian economy in the late nineteenth century when she was born, she saw the ascendancy of the industrial, capitalist system. Machines and systems of production have replaced much rough manual labor. Now as we enter the information age, we stand at the dawn of yet another transformation of work. Nevertheless, the Gospel challenge remains: How does our work cocreate the Reign of God; how is our work helping us be holy, healthy, and whole?

✧ Dorothy believed that our work can be holy, an extension of God's creative life in us. Reflect on the ways you are creative. Where are your talents centered? Express your thanks to God for the talents you possess and ask for the grace to use them wisely for the good of all creation.

✧ Dorothy believed that whatever our work, it should contribute to the common good. How does your work at home, on the farm, in an office or factory, or any volunteer work you do fit into Dorothy's criteria that our work should always be related to the works of mercy?

✧ The idea of working with one's hands, manual labor, held a privileged position in the Benedictine tradition of "prayer and work," and for Dorothy and Peter. Consider the many ways you use your hands on your job, in work around the house, in a craft or hobby. Thank God for the gift of manual work.

✧ Dorothy deeply appreciated Saint Joseph, the patron saint of workers. Read over the middle passage in Dorothy's Words and let your imagination recreate the scene in the "crude carpenter shop of Nazareth." Picture the relationship of Joseph and the young Jesus, and imagine the lessons given as Joseph coached Jesus. Ponder the manner in which you teach, coach, or supervise the work of other people. Do you treat other workers or those you supervise as you imagine Joseph would treat Jesus? Ask for Saint Joseph's assistance on these occasions.

✧ Many of the injustices and dangers in the workplace that Dorothy addressed in her writings continue today. Certainly not everyone is employed or privileged to do meaningful work in a safe environment and earn a living wage. Just as Dorothy wrote about the conditions she saw or learned about,

write in your journal, perhaps formatted as a letter or article being submitted to Dorothy the editor, about issues of your work, of work and working conditions in your area, or conditions in other countries. Consider sending your writing as a letter to the editor of your local paper.

God's Word

God said, "Let us make human beings in our own image, in the likeness of ourself." . . . God created human beings in God's own image, in the image of God they were created, male and female God created them. . . . God blessed them. . . . And so it was, looking at all of creation, God recognized it as very good. (Adapted from Genesis 1:26–31)

Closing prayer:

God . . . ,
creator and ruler of the universe,
in every age you call [people]
to develop and use [their] gifts for the good of others.
With St. Joseph as our example and guide,
help us to do the work you have asked
and come to the rewards you have promised.
("Prayer for the Feast of Joseph the Worker,"
The Roman Missal)

Living Voluntary Poverty

Theme: Embracing the Gospel invitation to become poor frees us to experience the unsurpassed richness of God's love.

Opening prayer: God of love, prepare my heart to learn how I might serve your poor ones through sharing with them the goods you have given me.

About Dorothy

Following Jesus' example and teaching, Dorothy chose voluntary poverty:

> Christ told Peter to put aside his nets and follow him. He told the rich young man to sell what he had and give to the poor and follow Him. He said that those who lost their lives for His sake should find them. He told his followers that if anyone begged for their coats to give up their cloaks, too. (*House of Hospitality*, p. 69)

Dorothy adopted this counsel for herself and made it a cornerstone of the Catholic Worker Movement.

Although Dorothy lived voluntary poverty as a way of responding to the Gospel, her attraction to it began earlier. When she was eighteen years old, Dorothy moved to New York City with her family. Her father, John Day, covered racing for the sports page of the *Morning Telegraph.* Dorothy looked for work as a journalist for five months with no luck. While job-hunting, she explored New York's neighborhoods by bus, streetcar, the subway, and on foot. The poverty she saw appalled her. The noise and dank smells coming from tenements assaulted her senses.

Finally, Dorothy convinced the editor of the *Call*, a radical paper of the time, to hire her to do a series of stories about herself as a one person "diet squad." She was going to demonstrate how to live on five dollars a week in spite of the high cost of living in the city. Dorothy found a furnished apartment in a tenement and bravely set out on this adventure in voluntary poverty. The apartment proved to be drafty, vermin- and bedbug-infested, and smelly, with howling cats in the halls at night. But Dorothy reveled in her newfound independence and the opportunity to be a journalist. She discovered that she could get a meal of bean soup, bread, and butter for ten cents and relied on some lunches bought by journalist friends. After three weeks, the series ended with the headline, "*Call's* Diet Squad Officially Reports System Won't Work" (Anne Klejment and Alice Klejment, *Dorothy Day and "The Catholic Worker,"* p. 8).

At age eighteen, Dorothy's sense of being drawn to share the life of poor people came from her keen sensitivity to her surroundings and the avant-garde ideas of her socialist friends. At the time, she had no idea of the Gospel invitation to become poor. She saw it as "the natural virtue of voluntary poverty" (*Long Loneliness*, p. 87).

Eventually, Peter Maurin taught Dorothy the spiritual power of voluntary poverty. Dorothy said of Peter, "He was a St. Francis of modern times" (p. 273). Peter viewed the voluntary poverty of Saint Francis of Assisi as a liberating force that made us "as free as the birds" if only we gave up all superfluous possessions. Peter practiced what he preached. He spent the night on a park bench if someone begged for the last of his money. He gave away his coat, and if someone else needed one, he begged for another. Peter insisted that nobody would be poor if everyone tried to be the poorest. Dorothy remarked:

> He never refused to give alms, no matter how poor he was. He believed in poverty and loved it and felt it a lib-

erating force. He differentiated between poverty and destitution, but the two often came close together in his life, when to give to others he had to strip himself. (P. 179)

Pause: Who do you know that has modeled voluntary poverty?

Dorothy's Words

It is hard to write about poverty.

. . . I had occasion to visit the city shelter last month where homeless families are cared for. I sat there for a couple of hours, contemplating poverty and destitution— a family with two of the children asleep in the parents' arms and four others sprawling against them; another young couple, the mother pregnant. I made myself known to a young man in charge. (I did not want to appear to be spying on them when all I wanted to know was the latest on the apartment situation for homeless families.) He apologized for making me wait, explaining that he had thought I was one of the clients.

We need always to be thinking and writing about poverty, for if we are not among its victims its reality fades from us. We must talk about poverty, because people insulated by their own comfort lose sight of it. . . .

And maybe no one can be told; maybe they will have to experience it. Or maybe it is a grace which they must pray for. We usually get what we pray for, and maybe we are afraid to pray for it. And yet I am convinced that it is the grace we most need in this age of crisis, this time when expenditures reach into the billions to defend "our American way of life." Maybe this defense itself will bring down upon us the poverty we are afraid to pray for. . . .

No one working with *The Catholic Worker* gets a salary, so our readers feel called upon to give and help us keep the work going. And then we experience a poverty of another kind, a poverty of reputation. It is said often and with some scorn, "Why don't they get jobs and help the poor that way? Why are they living off others, begging?"

I can only explain to such critics that it would complicate things to give a salary to Roger for his work of fourteen hours a day in the kitchen, clothes room, and office; to pay Jane a salary for running the women's house and Beth and Annabelle for giving out clothes, for making stencils all day and helping with the sick and the poor, and then have them all turn the money right back in to support the work. . . . It is simpler just to be poor. It is simpler to beg. The main thing is not to hold on to anything.

But the tragedy is that we do, we all do hold on—to our books, our tools, such as typewriters, our clothes; and instead of rejoicing when they are taken from us we lament. We protest when people take our time or privacy. We are holding on to these "goods" too. . . .

Voluntary poverty, Peter Maurin would say, is the answer. Through voluntary poverty we will have the means to help our brothers. We cannot even see our brothers in need without first stripping ourselves. It is the only way we have of showing our love. (Dorothy Day, "Poverty and Precarity," *The Catholic Worker*, May 1952)

Reflection

Once while writing about voluntary poverty Dorothy exclaimed, "No, it is not simple, this business of poverty" (*The Catholic Worker*, May 1952). She had in mind the many mixed motives one might have in choosing voluntary poverty or a poorer lifestyle. She knew that sometimes a certain romantic idealism can overtake us about poverty, not unlike her own idealism when she was eighteen years old. On a purely natural level, we might yearn for the simple life, free of responsibility and care, dependent on the fruits of others' labor.

Dorothy knew that voluntary poverty is a profound critique of the prevailing American way of life with its emphasis on security, acquisitiveness, material possessions, and wealth in general. She also knew that Catholic Worker voluntary poverty would challenge her own church, so often scandalously wealthy. And finally, she knew that those who choose voluntary poverty, Catholic Worker-style, enter a purifying experi ence not unlike the early Christians who sought holiness by venturing into the desert. Voluntary poverty profoundly challenges anyone with some security and a superfluity of possessions.

Dorothy and Peter often distinguished poverty, voluntary or involuntary, from destitution. They recognized that all people need a certain amount of the goods of this earth for a good life. Those that can work to support themselves and their families should do so and not live off someone else's labor. Beauty and enjoyment are also necessary for a dignified life. Dorothy loved driving the used cars donated to the Catholic Worker Movement, enjoyed being treated to lunch, and relished listening to the opera on the radio. Poverty does not mean abundance, but it has a human face. On the other hand, destitution means squalor, filth, disease, hunger, homelessness, and ugliness. Destitution can rob people of their human dignity.

Jesus and Dorothy remind us to ponder voluntary poverty. In the following reflections, approach voluntary poverty on a "What if . . ." basis: What if I did choose to live a life of voluntary poverty? We might proceed along this "what if" path in a series of steps, each moving us closer to the Gospel and Dorothy's ideal. Let each of your reflections pass through the prism of your responsibilities to others and to your profession. But let your reflections on voluntary poverty shed a new light on the lifestyle you may now take for granted.

✧ Do you find a life of voluntary poverty at all attractive? If so, why? If not, why not? Does the freedom of simple living, the challenge of Christ, the witness of some saint, the desire to serve the poor, or some other motive move you to voluntary poverty? Write your responses to these questions in your journal.

✧ Dorothy understood that personal efforts begin with small steps:

On the one hand it begins with the little sacrifices—doing without something in order to help others, whether it is clothes or food and drink. Then, just as Jesus Christ took the small boy's loaves and fishes, He multiplies our small works. He opens the way to us to do more and more. (Dorothy Day, "We Know What Poverty Is," *Witness*, 4 December 1966, p. 3)

Consider what might be superfluous in your lifestyle right now. What things or habits might you let go?

✧ Dorothy often spoke of "precarity" as opposed to security. Few today have real security; many of us live in some degree of precariousness. What if you were forced to cut back by the loss of a job or an illness. How would your life change? Draw up a budget based on 80 percent, 60 percent, or 40 percent of your current income. Would you really be worse off? What opportunities might open up with less money?

✧ Consider voluntary poverty as the antidote to the spirit of acquisitiveness that always believes we do not have enough. Make a list of alternatives to your accustomed patterns of consumption. How would your recreation and enjoyment change if you lived on less? What positive gains would emerge? What if you altered patterns of consuming by, for example, canceling cable TV and reading more books, phoning long distance less and writing more personal letters? As you reflect, remember that voluntary poverty for Saint Francis, Peter Maurin, and Dorothy Day was not destitution; it was full of joy and freedom.

✧ Dorothy understood how easy it is to hold on to our possessions, especially the nonmaterial ones such as time, privacy, and reputation. Do you hold onto these possessions too tightly? If so, how might you release that holding-on attitude?

✧ If you were to move from "what if" and imagination to action, what fears or internal objections would have to be overcome? After you have collected your fears and objections, meditate on Dorothy's words: "The wonderful thing is that each one of us can do something about the problem, . . . and God 'ordereth all things sweetly,' and there is no need to be afraid as to where such a response will lead us" (Dorothy Day, "The Meaning of Poverty," *Ave Maria*, 3 December 1966, p. 29).

✧ Ponder the scriptural images in God's Word. Dwell on one image or phrase you are drawn to. Do as Jesus suggests: look at the birds and consider the flowers. Accept Dorothy's challenge to pray for the grace of voluntary poverty.

God's Word

Stop worrying so much about what your next meal will be, about how your body looks, or about dressing in fashion. Human life is more than food. Your body is worth more than the clothes draped on it. Watch the birds. Notice that they do not plant crops or store grain in silos, but the Creator gives them food. You are worth more than birds, aren't you? Can you add one second to your life by fretting about it? No. And why are you obsessed with clothing? The marvelous wildflowers do not sew or weave, but not even Solomon with all his wealth was arrayed as beautifully as a wildflower. So if God loves flowers so much, even though they wither and die in one season, don't you think the Creator loves you more? . . . God knows what you need. Turn your heart and focus your attention on building the Reign of God in your midst. The necessities will be given to you as well. Do not worry about tomorrow; tomorrow will fend for itself. Each day has sufficient trouble of its own. (Adapted from Matthew 6:25–34)

Closing prayer:

Happy those who have regard for the lowly and the poor.
The Most Holy will regard them and preserve them.
And make them happy on the earth.

(Adapted from Psalm 41)

Active Love

Theme: Active love of our neighbor, Dorothy understood, is certainly not always easy. But through active love, God's life and power manifests itself within us and to other people.

Opening prayer: Kind God, turn my desire to love you and my neighbor into action. Reveal the mystery of your love for me in my love of neighbor, and sustain me in that love all the days of my life.

About Dorothy

Dorothy referred to these words of Father Zosima, a character in Fyodor Dostoyevsky's *The Brothers Karamazov,* many times in her life: "Active love is a harsh and fearful thing compared with love in dreams" (p. 58). She treasured all of Dostoyevsky's works, reading and rereading them many times. However, these words of Father Zosima were burned into her soul and came to represent one of the cornerstones of her vision. But before she could enter into the mystery and practice of active love in her life, Dorothy first discovered love in dreams.

As a young woman of fifteen living in Chicago, Dorothy experienced the first distant call to active love. She was avidly reading the socially conscious literature of Carl Sandburg, Jack London, and Upton Sinclair, and it stirred her imagination.

I walked for miles, pushing my brother in his carriage, often with my sister at my side, she usually holding onto the carriage too. We explored until we were footsore, going up and down interminable gray streets, fascinating in their dreary sameness, past tavern after tavern, where I envisaged such scenes as that of the Polish wedding party in Sinclair's story, past houses which were sunk down a whole story below street level for block after block. . . .

. . . Though my only experience of the destitute was in books, the very fact that *The Jungle* was about Chicago where I lived, whose streets I walked, made me feel that from then on my life was to be linked to theirs, their interests were to be mine; I had received a call, a vocation, a direction to my life.

I felt even at fifteen, that God meant man to be happy, that He meant to provide him with what he needed to maintain life in order to be happy, and that we did not need to have quite so much destitution and misery as I saw all around and read of in the daily press. (*Long Loneliness*, pp. 37–38)

In her dreams and imagination, Dorothy identified with the plight of the masses and the social conditions around her. Her love became active, personal, and concrete when she started the Catholic Worker Movement.

Her beloved Dostoyevsky character Father Zosima prefigured what happened to Dorothy's love when she began to live in the Catholic Worker houses of hospitality. Father Zosima says:

Active love is a harsh and fearful thing compared with love in dreams. Love in dreams thirsts for immediate action, quickly performed, and with everyone watching. Indeed, it will go so far as the giving even of one's life, provided it does not take long but is soon over, as on stage, and everyone is looking on and praising. Whereas active love is labor and perseverance, and for some people, perhaps, a whole science. But I predict that even in that very moment when you see with horror that despite all your efforts, you not only have not come nearer your goal but seem to have gotten farther from it, at that very moment—I predict this to you—you will suddenly reach your goal and will clearly behold over you the wonder-working power of the Lord, who all the while has been loving you, and all the while has been mysteriously guiding you. (Fyodor Dostoyevsky, *The Brothers Karamazov*, p. 58)

Pause: Have you known love in dreams and experienced the harshness of active love? Have you also experienced the wonder-working power of God?

Dorothy's Words

During World War II, critics accused Dorothy and the Catholic Worker Movement of being afraid of suffering and the hardships of war. One newspaper sympathized with what they perceived as her naive sentimentality. Dorothy responded:

> But let those who talk of softness, of sentimentality, come to live with us in cold, unheated houses in the slums. Let them come to live with the criminal, the unbalanced, the drunken, the degraded, the perverted. (It is not decent poor, it is not the decent sinner who was the recipient of Christ's love.) Let them live with rats, with vermin, bedbugs, roaches, lice (I could describe the several kinds of body lice).
>
> Let their flesh be mortified by cold, by dirt, by vermin; let their eyes be mortified by the sight of bodily excretions, diseased limbs, eyes, noses, mouths.
>
> Let their noses be mortified by the smells of sewage, decay, and rotten flesh. Yes, and the smell of sweat, blood, and tears spoken of so blithely by Mr. Churchill, and so widely and bravely quoted by comfortable people.
>
> Let their ears be mortified by harsh and screaming voices, by the constant coming and going of people living herded together with no privacy.
>
> Let their taste be mortified by the constant eating of insufficient food cooked in huge quantities for hundreds of people, the coarser foods, so that there will be enough to go around; and the smell of such cooking is often foul.

Then when they have lived with these comrades, with these sights and sounds, let our critics talk of sentimentality. As we have often quoted Dostoevsky's Father Zossima, "Love in practice is a harsh and dreadful thing compared to love in dreams." (*The Catholic Worker*, February 1942)

Reflection

Active love was part of Dorothy's daily experience in the Catholic Worker houses of hospitality and farms where she lived. She loved in practice by responding immediately to the neighbor at hand, by taking personal responsibility to do what could be done, often with no gratitude or permanent results. Over the years this experience served like a refiner's fire, at once testing her endurance but ultimately transforming her love of neighbor and her love of God.

As we reflect on active love in our life, we need to consider two key aspects of active love: "Love in dreams" is often a necessary stage before we can love actively; and many, if not all of us, have or will have the opportunity to experience the harsh aspects of active love.

✧ Consider how "love in dreams" has been present in your life, perhaps writing your reflections in your journal or as a letter to Dorothy Day:
+ Recall times in your life when you were filled with idealism for a cause.
+ List scripture passages, words from a sermon, some passage you may have read, or an image that inspired you and moved you to desire to act or help in some way.

✧ Part of active love is seeing the opportunities for it in our immediate surroundings, in the place where we live. Take a walk around your neighborhood or a neighborhood near you—like Dorothy's walk with her brother in the stroller. Activate your imagination to see behind the facade of dwellings and consider how the need for active love is hidden in them. Imagine the people inside, what their life must be like, how they might need active love.

✧ In the passage from Dostoyevsky in About Dorothy, the character Father Zosima is trying to give assurance to a woman who felt that she needed to be rewarded in helping the poor. Read Father Zosima's words again and carefully consider the qualities of active love described: labor and perseverance, "a whole science" of active love, discouragement and apparent failure, the appearance of the power of God who is loving you. Compare this to love in dreams.

✧ How have you experienced the harshness of active love? Perhaps you care for your aging parents, or struggle with abuse or addiction in a relationship, or work in a profession where you see the victims of violence, poverty, and neglect. Have you smelled, seen, and heard the kinds of things about which Dorothy writes? Have you been discouraged? How have you gotten through it? Have you experienced the "wonder-working power" of God in your apparent failures? Pray the opening or closing prayer from this meditation now and whenever discouragement in love is present.

✧ What fears do you have about the harsh side of active love? Do you fear for your safety, that you might be exposed to disease, that you will be rejected, that you will receive slurs, even that you might be sued? Meditate on the words of Saint Paul on ministry in God's Word.

God's Word

We avoid putting obstacles in anyone's way, so that no blame may attach our work of service; but in everything we prove ourselves authentic servants of God; by resolute perseverance in times of hardships, difficulties and distress; when we are flogged or sent to prison or mobbed; labouring sleepless, starving; in purity, in knowledge, in patience, in kindness; in the Holy Spirit, in a love free of affectation; in the word of truth and in the power of God. (2 Corinthians 6:3–7)

Closing prayer: Gracious God, look upon me in my efforts to love my neighbor. Strengthen me when I am unsure of myself and my love of you. Sustain me in my efforts to love you in my neighbor. Make my love concrete and active. Reveal to me the mystery of your presence in my actions for those who I am called to serve.

The Little Way

Theme: The little, ordinary acts of everyday experience contain a power of love that can transform us and the whole world. Thérèse of Lisieux called this the "Little Way," and Dorothy took this way to heart.

Opening prayer: God, increase my desire to love you in all that I am and do. Help me appreciate your presence in each moment and experience of today. Let me join my Little Way with Jesus' cross so that we might renew the face of the earth.

About Dorothy

Dorothy was ecstatic over the birth of her daughter, whom she decided to name Tamar Teresa: Tamar after a dear friend's little girl and Teresa after Saint Teresa of Ávila, one of the few Christian saints Dorothy had heard of. When Dorothy told the young Catholic woman in the next bed the name, the woman exclaimed "And Teresa is after the Little Flower?" (Dorothy Day, *Therese*, p. vi). She gave Dorothy a medal of the Little Flower for the baby, but Dorothy shied away from it. Not yet a Catholic, Dorothy saw the medal as evidence of superstition and charm-wearing. She was concerned that the baby might swallow the medal or that the pin would come loose and pierce her. However, Dorothy found a way to accept both saints, Teresa of Ávila and Thérèse of Lisieux:

I decided that although I would name my child after the older saint, the new one would be my own Teresa's novice mistress, to train her in the spiritual life. I knew that I wanted to have the child baptized a Catholic and I wanted both saints to be taking care of her. One was not enough. (Pp. vi–vii)

Two years later, and only a year after her baptism as a Catholic, Dorothy was given Thérèse of Lisieux's autobiography to read by her confessor, Father Zachary, who told her, "Here is a book that will do you good."

I dutifully read *The Story of a Soul* and am ashamed to confess that I found it colorless, monotonous, too small in fact for my notice. What kind of a saint was this who felt that she had to practice heroic charity in eating what was put in front of her, in taking medicine, enduring cold and heat, restraint, enduring the society of mediocre souls, in following the strict regime of the convent of Carmelite nuns which she had joined at the age of fifteen? (P. viii)

Dorothy thought the book vacuously pious and an insult to her intelligence. She told Father Zachary that her concept of a saint was more heroic and that Thérèse's way did not quite fit this time of world revolution. The year was 1928.

Thirty years later, her opinion had completely turned around. In the introduction to her biography of Thérèse, Dorothy says that she wanted to introduce her readers to a saint of our day. By this time in her life, Dorothy had come to understand Thérèse's Little Way. Life with the Catholic Worker Movement, the daily practice of the works of mercy, the year-in and year-out contact with poor and destitute people, and the struggle for peace and justice schooled Dorothy in the meaning of the Little Way.

Dorothy believed that Thérèse's Little Way was open to everyone, whatever their situation in life:

I wrote to overcome the sense of futility in Catholics, men, women, and youths, married and single, who feel hopeless and useless, less than the dust, ineffectual, wasted, powerless. On the one hand Therese was "the little grain of sand" and on the other "her name was written in heaven"; she was beloved by her heavenly Father, she was the bride of Christ, she was little less than the angels. And so are we all. (*Therese*, p. xii)

Pause: Ponder this question for a moment: Can I really live a holy life by doing all the little deeds of my days with care and faith?

Dorothy's Words

Yet it was the "worker," the common man, who first spread [Thérèse's] fame by word of mouth. It was the masses who first proclaimed her a saint. It was the "people."

When we think of the masses, we think of waves of the sea, of forests, of fields of wheat, all moved by the spirit which blows where it listeth. When we think of the people we think of the child at school, the housewife at her dishpan, the mother working, the mother sick, the man traveling, the migrant worker, the craftsman, the factory worker, the soldier, the rich, the bourgeois, the poor in tenements, the destitute man in the street. To a great extent she has made her appeal to all of these.

What was there about her to make such an appeal? Perhaps because she was so much like the rest of us in her ordinariness. In her lifetime there are no miracles recounted, she was just good, good as the bread which the Normans bake in huge loaves, and which makes up such a large part of their diet. . . .

What did she do? She practiced the presence of God and she did all things—all the little things that make up our daily life and contact with others—for His honor and glory. . . .

She speaks to our condition. Is the atom a small thing? And yet what havoc it has wrought. Is her little way a small contribution to the life of the spirit? It has all the power of the spirit of Christianity behind it. It is an explosive force that can transform our lives and the life of the world, once put into effect. . . .

The mystery of suffering has a different aspect under the New Covenant, since Christ died on the Cross and took on Himself men's sins. Now St. Paul teaches that we can fill up the sufferings of Christ, that we must share in the sufferings of the world to lessen them, to show our love for our brothers. But God does not change, so we can trust with Abraham that for even ten just men, He will not destroy the city. We can look with faith and hope to that *mighty army of little ones* that St. Therese has promised us and which is present now among us. (*Therese*, pp. 173–176)

Reflection

Thérèse of Lisieux's spirituality in its entirety is still being explored for its depth, power, and subtlety by writers and theologians. Her Little Way affirms what many ordinary people suspect but often discount: Holiness consists in doing ordinary acts with love, attention, respect, and hope; it means seeing Christ in everyone and serving Christ in all our little acts.

Dorothy's identification with Thérèse's Little Way came from within her experience and Catholic Worker vocation. When she chose to write *Therese*, Dorothy knew many other biographies of the saint existed. Dorothy says about her book, "It is written very much from my own point of view, emphasizing aspects of her life, and of her family's life, that interested me particularly" (p. x). Consequently, these reflections on the Little Way focus on those aspects of Thérèse's spirituality that were especially important to Dorothy. The reflections invite us to go along the Little Way.

✧ Dorothy wrote "We are all called to be saints, St. Paul says, and we might as well get over our bourgeois fear of the name" (Robert Ellsberg, ed., *By Little and By Little: The Selected Writings of Dorothy Day*, pp. 102–103). What images come to mind when you think of a saint? Consider some saints you have heard of or know something about. What qualities of Christ do they exemplify? Like Dorothy, have you re-evaluated your view of their life? What might it mean to your life that you are called to be a saint? Write in your journal about what kind of a saint you might be.

✧ Dorothy summed up Thérèse's Little Way in these words: "She called it little because it partakes of the simplicity of a child, a very little child, in its attitude of abandonment, of acceptance" (*Therese*, p. 154). For Dorothy and Thérèse, the Little Way meant trusting God as the intimate and deepest source of love and power for good. Jesus admonished his followers to become like a little child. How might you grow in an appreciation of this truth? Spend some time with a little child or go to a playground and observe children playing. Does anything stand in your way of having this tender relationship with God? Pray to know more about this mystery.

✧ The Little Way includes learning to be dependent on God, especially when we might become discouraged.

> Today we are not content with little achievements, with small beginnings. We should look to St. Teresa, the Little Flower, to walk her little way, her way of love. . . .
> . . . Whatsoever thy hand finds to do, do it with all thy might. After all, God is with us. It shows too much conceit to trust to ourselves, to be discouraged at what we ourselves can accomplish. It is lacking in faith in God to be discouraged. (*House of Hospitality*, p. 64)

Are you discouraged about something? What is at hand today for you to do? Focus on the here and now and just do what you can. Ask for God's help today in what lies before you.

✧ Dorothy saw that even the smallest acts of love have tremendous power. Read Dorothy's Words again, slowly and reflectively, especially her image of the tiny atom and its power. Visualize that "mighty army of little ones." Meditate on how small acts of love you have done, and might do, can ripple through the world.

✧ The Little Way can also be called the "ordinary way." In the sacrament of the here and now, we can practice the presence of God and ask, like Thérèse, "What would He have me to do?" (*Therese*, p. 69). What choices will you face in the next hour? Ask God, "What would you have me do?"

As you go about your day, pause from time to time and enter into the spirit of the Little Way. Repeat the phrase "What would you have me do?" as a prayer.

✧ Martyrs give their lives for Christ and are joined to the martyrdom of the cross. Thérèse's Little Way is the martyrdom of ordinary life: losing a job, bearing pain, feeling weak, living in loneliness. On these occasions, we can fill up the sufferings of Christ. Read and meditate on Dorothy's Words again. Consider the passage in God's Word from Saint Paul and its promise; then ask for an increase in faith and hope.

God's Word

Everything is for your benefit, so that as grace spreads, so, to the glory of God, thanksgiving may also overflow among more and more people.

That is why we do not waver; indeed, though this outer human nature of ours may be falling into decay, at the same time our inner human nature is renewed day by day. The temporary, light burden of our hardships is earning us for ever an utterly incomparable, eternal weight of glory. (2 Corinthians 4:15–17)

Closing prayer: God, may I feel your presence today, especially in the ordinary moments. To say I want to be a saint is not easy. But little by little and day by day, I want to increase my love of you and, with your help, bring that love to those I will meet today. I am grateful to your friends, Thérèse and Dorothy, for showing me the Little Way.

Enduring in Faith

Theme: Dorothy believed that to remain faithful to her vocation she had to identify with poor people. Doing so enabled her to believe in love.

Opening prayer: Faithful God, strengthen my faith in you and help me to enter into your love for me when I love others.

About Dorothy

Dorothy sat at the supper table at Saint Joseph's House and looked around the room. Now sixty-seven years old, she was certainly familiar with the scene after all these years of the Catholic Worker Movement. But something prompted her to look at her surroundings with the eye of a visitor entering the room for the first time. The place looked dingy. There were yellow walls, icon-like paintings on wood, and once colorful banners, now faded. A large, gilded iron crucifix someone had donated adorned one end of the room. As usual, the place was warm, informal, and noisy with conversation, but the poor men, women, and children sitting there bore the marks of misery and destitution.

As Dorothy surveyed the scene, the hard questions that she had heard many times from visitors echoed in her momentary reflection:

"Aren't we deceiving ourselves, I am sure many of them think, in the work we are doing? What are we accomplishing for them anyway, or for the world or for the common good? 'Are these people being rehabilitated?' is the question we get almost daily from visitors or from our readers." (*The Catholic Worker*, April 1964)

These and other questions came not only from visitors but sprang from inside Dorothy too.

Pause: Ask yourself: What am I accomplishing for the common good?

Dorothy's Words

One priest had his catechism classes write us questions as to our work after they had the assignment in religion class to read my book *The Long Loneliness*. The majority of them asked the same question: "How can you see Christ in people?" And we only say: It is an act of faith, constantly repeated. It is an act of love, resulting from an act of faith. It is an act of hope, that we can awake these same acts in their hearts, too, with the help of God, and the Works of Mercy, which you, our readers, help us to do, day in and day out over the years.

On Easter Day, on awakening late after the long midnight services in our parish church, I read over the last chapter of the four Gospels and felt that I received great light and understanding with the reading of them. "They have taken the Lord out of His tomb and we do not know where they have laid Him," Mary Magdalene said, and we can say this with her in times of doubt and questioning. How do we know we believe? How do we know we indeed have faith? Because we have seen His hands and His feet in the poor around us. He has shown Himself to us in them. We start by loving them for Him, and we soon love them for themselves, each one a unique person, most special! . . .

How can I help but think of these things every time I sit down at Chrystie Street or Peter Maurin Farm and look around at the tables filled with the unutterably poor who are going through their long-continuing crucifixion. It is most surely an exercise of faith for us to see Christ in each other. But it is through such exercise that we grow and the joy of our vocation assures us we are on the right path.

Most certainly, it is easier to believe now that the sun warms us, and we know that buds will appear on the sycamore trees in the wasteland across from the Catholic Worker office, that life will spring out of the dull clods of that littered park across the way. There are wars and rumors of war, poverty and plague, hunger and pain. Still, the sap is rising, again there is the resurrection of spring, God's continuing promise to us that He is with us always, with His comfort and joy, if we will only ask.

The mystery of the poor is this: That they are Jesus, and what you do for them you do for Him. It is the only way we have of knowing and believing in our love. The mystery of poverty is that by sharing in it, making ourselves poor in giving to others, we increase our knowledge of and belief in love. (*The Catholic Worker*, April 1964)

Reflection

Dorothy chose to identify with poor people and serve them through the works of mercy. Faith called her to this way of life, and she followed. Not surprisingly, she sometimes wondered if it had all been worthwhile. Year after year, despite her best efforts, more poor people needed food, clothing, and shelter. Year after year, violence stalked the earth. Year after year, greed, racism, sexism, and injustice divided the human family.

Even though we may be committed to the Little Way, desiring large, tangible results always tempts us. In her bleaker moments, Dorothy was also tempted. Like Dorothy, when we stop and look at our life choices so far, we might also wonder if we have been deceiving ourselves, and we may need reassurance in our love.

Dorothy believed that when we love poor people, we are loving Christ directly. A poor person is not a stand-in for Christ; neither have we gone through some mental substitution that superimposes Christ's face over the poor person's like a mask. But even Dorothy had to remind herself of Christ's presence there. Thus, she meditated on the real lives of poor people. Their courage and faith often inspired and encouraged her. Their faith and hope inflamed and renewed her faith and hope.

Throughout her life Dorothy received great strength from the words of scripture and from prayer. The combination of active love of God's *anawim*, or little ones, meditation, and prayer renewed her and helped her endure inner doubts and outer pressures.

✧ Have you ever doubted the path you have chosen or the efficacy of your efforts? Write about these doubts in your journal. Read God's Word in this meditation or open your Bible to a favorite scriptural passage that strengthens you. Read it slowly and prayerfully. If a particular word or phrase stands out, repeat it slowly in rhythm with your breathing.

✧ Springtime outside her window gave Dorothy a fresh sense of hope. Go to a place where you can experience the wonder of renewed life with your senses. If possible go to a garden or a park where children play. Place yourself in the presence of an infant, or just get up early to greet the sunrise. Drink in the wonder of the moment. Express your thanks to God for this sign of life.

✧ How do you measure the success of your life's endeavors? Examine your attitudes by listing your criteria for success in such areas as your work, your relationships with others, your faith, and even your whole life. Dorothy often spoke of embracing Saint Paul's notion of the "folly of the cross" as expressing the heart of the mystery of Christ. Reflect on how this attitude is in conflict with our culture's or your notions of success.

✧ Slowly read Dorothy's Words again and ponder the fact that in serving needy people, we also serve Christ. Then ask yourself: If I really believe this, how can I doubt the goodness of even small acts of service?

✧ Spend some time with someone in need. This could be a materially poor person or someone poor in spirit because of illness, loneliness, failure, or grief. Express your love for them through one of the corporal or spiritual works of mercy.

God's Word

Friend, when difficulties confront you, be joyful. These troubles test your faith, but can produce endurance. This perseverance grows into rich faith with which you can face anything. (Adapted from James 1:2–3)

Closing prayer: Merciful God, you call me to walk in the way of Christ. Free me from fear, doubt, and anxiety, and guard me in the radiance of your truth.

Peacemakers

Theme: The Gospel calls all of us to be peacemakers and people of nonviolence.

Opening prayer: Holy Friend, our world is still full of hate, violence, and war. Help us now to take to heart your commandment to love our enemies. May we become your blessed peacemakers.

About Dorothy

Dorothy and a small group of people sat on the park benches across from New York's City Hall on a spring day in 1955. The wail of sirens signaled the beginning of the air-raid drill, sending millions scurrying into subway tunnels. Office workers hurried to fallout shelters in buildings, and fearful children hastened to crouch beneath their school desks. Everyone was supposed to take shelter, but Dorothy and her friends just sat there in the park, handing a leaflet to those who would take one. For Dorothy, the Cold War was utter folly and reliance on nuclear weapons a futile strategy, the ultimate disrespect for human life.

The quiet protest gave a loud and prophetic witness to the violence implied in atomic weapons, the most terrible war-making weapons yet devised. The Catholic Worker leaflet that day included these words: "In the name of Jesus, who is God, who is Love, we will not obey this order to pretend, to evacuate, to hide. . . . We will not be drilled into fear. . . . We do not have faith in God if we depend upon the Atom Bomb" (Jim Forest, *Love Is the Measure*, p. 135).

Police arrested the group, and that first year Dorothy stayed a single night in jail. When the protest was repeated the next year, Dorothy spent five days in jail. In the following year, 1957, she endured a difficult and exhausting thirty-day sentence in the Women's House of Detention.

Many people asked what purpose this protest served. Dorothy responded this way:

> It is a gesture, perhaps, but a necessary one. Silence means consent, and we cannot consent to the militarization of our country without protest. Since we believe that air raid drills are part of a calculated plan to inspire fear of the enemy, instead of the love which Jesus Christ told us we should feel, we must protest these drills. It is an opportunity to show we mean what we write when we repeat over and over that we are put here on this earth to love God and our neighbor. (P. 137)

For Dorothy, this act of civil disobedience was an act of faithfulness to the Gospel.

Over the next four years more people joined the civil disobedience in City Hall Park. Two thousand people gathered in 1961, the last year New York had civil defense drills.

Pause: Ask yourself: How am I a peacemaker?

Dorothy's Words

After the United States declared war on Japan, Dorothy wrote this letter in *The Catholic Worker* newspaper:

> Dear Fellow Workers in Christ:
> Lord God, merciful God, our Father, shall we keep silent, or shall we speak? And if we speak, what shall we say?

I am sitting here in the church on Mott Street writing this in Your presence. Out on the streets it is quiet, but You are there, too, in the Chinese, in the Italians, these neighbors we love. We love them because they are our brothers, as Christ is our Brother, and God our Father. . . .

Seventy-five thousand copies of *The Catholic Worker* go out every month. What shall we print? . . .

We will print the words of Christ, who is with us always, even to the end of the world. "Love your enemies, do good to those who hate you, and pray for those who persecute and calumniate you, so that you may be children of your Father in heaven, who makes His sun to rise on the good and the evil, and sends rain on the just and unjust. . . ."

We are still pacifists. Our manifesto is the Sermon on the Mount, which means that we will try to be peacemakers. Speaking for many of our conscientious objectors, we will not participate in armed warfare or in making munitions, or by buying government bonds to prosecute the war, or in urging others to these efforts.

But neither will we be carping in our criticism. We love our country and we love our President. We have been the only country in the world where men and women of all nations have taken refuge from oppression. We recognize that while in the order of intention we have tried to stand for peace, for love of our brothers and sisters, in the order of execution we have failed as Americans in living up to our principles. . . .

Let us add that unless we continue this prayer [for an end to war] with almsgiving, in giving to the least of God's children; and fasting in order that we may help feed the hungry; and penance in recognition of our share in the guilt, our prayer may become empty words.

Our Works of Mercy may take us into the midst of war. As editor of *The Catholic Worker*, I would urge our friends and associates to care for the sick and the wounded, to the growing of food for the hungry, to the continuance of all our Works of Mercy in our houses and on our farms. We understand, of course, that there is and that there will be great differences of opinion even among our own groups as to how much collaboration we can have with the government in times like these. There are differences more profound and there will be many continuing to work with us from necessity, or from choice, who do not agree with us as to our position on war, conscientious objection, etc. But we beg that there will be mutual charity and forbearance among us all.

Because of our refusal to assist in the prosecution of war and our insistence that our collaboration be one for peace, we may find ourselves in difficulties. But we trust in the generosity and understanding of our government and our friends, to permit us to continue, to use our paper to "preach Christ crucified." ("Our Country Passes from Undeclared to Declared War; We Continue Our Christian Pacifist Stand," January 1942)

Reflection

At the heart of Dorothy's lifelong commitment to peace was her unswerving conviction that God loves every human being unconditionally. That this love could want or condone the destruction of any person was simply unthinkable. The works of war stood directly opposite the works of mercy. And since we are all members of the Mystical Body of Christ, we should love our friends and our enemies.

Dorothy's witness, often alone and in the face of criticism, was finally recognized after her death. Eileen Egan writes:

She did not live long enough to see in May 1983 the 40,000-word pastoral letter of the U.S. bishops devoted solely to peace and war. *God's Promise and Our Response* contained a thousand-word section titled "The Value of Nonviolence," in which the bishops stated, "The nonviolent witness of such figures as Dorothy Day and Martin Luther King has had a profound effect upon the life of the Church in the United States." Dorothy Day's life-long commitment to peacemaking, despite misunderstanding, opposition and attack, was validated in the bishops'

declaration that "peacemaking is not an optional commitment; it is a requirement of faith." (Patrick G. Coy, ed., *A
Revolution of the Heart*, p. 108)

Dorothy reminded her readers that Christ, the Prince of
Peace, calls all Christians to be peacemakers, whether in dra-
matic or in small ways. Christ dwells in poor people, and he
also lives in our enemies. Thus, violence to them is violence
done to Christ. Peacemaking builds up the Body of Christ.

✧ Dorothy did not hesitate to be identified as a pacifist
opposed to all wars and violence. After all, pacifist comes
from the Latin words meaning "to make peace." To be a pacifist means to be a peacemaker and to oppose force and violence as a means of settling personal, societal, national, or
international conflicts.
✦ Examine your attitudes about the word "pacifist." Is there
any sense in which you might be a pacifist?
✦ Pray repeatedly Jesus' words from the Beatitudes, "Blessed
are the peacemakers." Say the words slowly and thought-
fully.
✦ Are there instances of violence in or near your life now—
domestic, urban, against the unborn—that require your
peacemaking?

✧ Reflect on these questions and dialog with Dorothy
and Christ about them:
✦ How do you feel about Dorothy's actions in protesting the
air raids?
✦ Dorothy wondered if she should speak out and what to say.
Have you felt compelled to break your silence about an is-
sue and wondered whether and what to say?
✦ Could you imagine yourself protesting publicly against
war, abortion, sexism, racism, injustice?
✦ Could you imagine going to jail for your conviction?
✦ Have you been concerned about being ridiculed or resist-
ed?

✧ Being a peacemaker includes the spiritual means of
prayer, fasting, giving alms, and performing works of mercy.

How might you do these peacemaking activities today in your setting? How might adoption be peacemaking? Might you make peace by helping support an immigrant in your town?

✧ Meditate on Jesus' strong words from the Sermon on the Mount that Dorothy quotes. Who might your enemies be? How has fear, real or imagined, numbed your heart? How might you love your enemies, removing the fear that blocks love?

✧ When you begin to use the language of "enemy" and feel the fear or anger that accompanies the term, try this exercise in personal peacemaking. Relax, breathe deeply, and picture your enemy in your mind's eye. In your imagination, surround your enemy with light. Call that light God's love, as it surely is in reality. Then place yourself within that circle of light. Imagine Jesus joining you in the circle. What does he say to you? Then ask God to let love penetrate both you and your enemy, bringing goodness and peace where you saw evil in your enemy and fear or anger in yourself.

Consider what actions you need to take to bring about reconciliation and peace with your enemy.

God's Word

"Blessed are the peacemakers:
they shall be recognized as children of God."

(Matthew 5:9)

Closing prayer:

In the midst of conflict and division,
we know it is you
who turn our minds to thoughts of peace.
Your Spirit changes our hearts:
enemies begin to speak to one another,
those who were estranged join hands in friendship,
and nations seek the way of peace together.

Your Spirit is at work
when understanding puts an end to strife,
when hatred is quenched by mercy,
and vengeance gives way to forgiveness.
(Eucharistic Prayer for Masses of Reconciliation II,
Eucharistic Prayers for Masses of Reconciliation)

✧ **Meditation 13** ✧

Thanksgiving

Theme: Deep joy is a gift to the thankful heart. Dorothy treasured God's gifts and gave voice to her gratitude.

Opening prayer: "Sing to God with thanksgiving; / sing praise with the harp to our God." (Psalm 147:7)

About Dorothy

A chill wind from the Thames River in Greenwich cut through Dorothy's light coat. She tucked a *London Times* newspaper inside her coat to protect against the cold. Sitting snugly now, she remarked to Eileen Egan, who had accompanied her to London, "I thank our men on the Bowery for teaching me this. We can all learn from one another" (Egan, *Permanent Revolution*, p. 17).

Dorothy's deep gratitude for all things, even tribulation, sprang from her deep conviction of God's love for the earth itself and all the people on it. Dorothy possessed a visceral knowledge of and thankfulness for God's providence. God gave gifts abundantly; all is gift.

Dorothy credited Forster for her love of the natural world. One day, sitting at the Staten Island shore at sunset, she found herself "praying with thanksgiving, praying with open eyes while I watched the workers on the beach and the sunset, and listened to the sound of the waves and the scream of snowy gulls" (*Long Loneliness*, p. 117). Although Dorothy lived most of her adulthood among the tenements and crowded dirty streets of New York's Lower East Side, scores of references to the natural world fill her writings. In many of her articles, before launching into her main point, she often commented on the sunlight, the changing season, a flower or tree, the smell of the ground itself.

Dorothy's daughter, Tamar, and her family inspired deep joy and gratitude in Dorothy. Although raising Tamar in the midst of the Catholic Worker Movement proved difficult at times, Dorothy never ceased being thankful for her. She delighted in helping Tamar and in spending time with her eight grandchildren.

A faithful Catholic, Dorothy gave deep thanks for the life of the Spirit she gained when she joined the church. Daily Mass and the Eucharist (the Greek word for thanksgiving) anchored Dorothy's soul to Christ and the Christian community.

The Catholic Worker Movement relied on the generosity of others to support its work, and Dorothy always tried to thank those who gave money, food, clothing, and household items. When a moose from Canada was offered, she refused it because they did not have proper storage, but at the same time she was delighted when someone dropped off two bottles of wine and a box of cigars one day.

On Dorothy's grave on Staten Island, near the scene of her conversion, her gravestone is inscribed with the words she wanted, "*Deo Gratias*," thanks be to God.

Pause: Ponder this question: For what am I thankful?

Dorothy's Words

The trees are getting bare, but still it stays warm. Coming down at night from the city, the warm, sweet smell of the good earth enwraps one like a garment. There is the smell of rotting apples; or alfalfa in the barn; burning leaves; of wood fires in the house; of pickled green tomatoes and baked beans.

Now there is a warm feeling of contentment about the farm these days—the first summer is over, many people have been cared for here, already. From day to day we did not know where the next money to pay bills was coming from, but trusting to our cooperators, our readers throughout the country, we went on with the work. Now all our bills are paid and there is a renewed feeling of courage on the part of all those who are doing the work, a sense of confidence that the work is progressing.

This month of thanksgiving will indeed be one of gratitude to God. For health, for work to do, for the opportunities He has given us of service; we are deeply grateful, and it is a feeling that makes the heart swell with joy.

During the summer when things were going especially hard in more ways than one, I grimly modified grace before meals: "We give Thee thanks, O Lord, for these Thy gifts, and for all our tribulations, from Thy bounty, through Christ our Lord, Amen." One could know of certain knowledge that tribulations were matters of thanksgiving; that we were indeed privileged to share in the sufferings of Our Lord. So in this month of thanksgiving, we can be thankful for the trials of the past, the blessings of the present, and be heartily ready at the same time to embrace with joy any troubles the future may bring us. (*The Catholic Worker*, November 1936)

Reflection

As Dorothy grew in wisdom, giving thanks became like breathing: it came naturally. When life is good, full of blessings and good things, giving thanks may come naturally for most of us too. Dorothy's thankfulness, however, encompasses the whole of life, the good and the inevitable trials and pain. In all circumstances, when thanks flows from a grateful heart, joy is the gift we receive. The grateful heart proclaims that God is lovingly present with us and gifts us with fullness of life. Even in suffering, God suffers with us, strengthens and supports us.

✧ Dorothy expressed profound thanks for the natural world, her faith, her family, and the generosity of other people toward her. How are you thankful for the natural world, your faith, your family, and the generosity you receive from others? Examine each area of gratefulness. How are each of these a gift of God?

✧ Focus on the place you call home. Through memory or direct observation, notice how the objects in your life are related to the earth, to family, to friends. Have you ever had to say thanks for a moose, some gift you would rather not deal with? On a piece of paper write the heading, "I am thankful for . . ." and quickly fill it with whatever comes to mind.

✧ Is there a particular person you are thankful for? Send them a letter or express your gratitude in another way that would be particularly delightful for them.

✧ Along with Saint Paul, Dorothy considered trials and tribulations as opportunities to share in the sufferings of Christ. Reflect on this question: Can I give thanks when all is not well? If this is such a time for you now, ask God for the grace to be thankful now and in the future.

✧ Dorothy understood that past, present, and future are all one in God and share in God's eternal goodness. From this perspective, thankfulness could reach back to the past, embrace the present, and anticipate all that God would provide in the future.
+ Reach back into your memories of childhood. Be thankful by praying, "God I thank you for . . ." (fill in the people, objects, and events that come to mind).
+ Imagine your future or what you hope will be. Give thanks in advance for God's loving providence for you.

✧ Sometimes the words "Thank You" are used as a public relations gesture without a lot of thought: for example, the store clerk who says, "Thank you for shopping at our store," or the TV anchor who says, "Thanks for watching. We'll see you tomorrow." Monitor your use of "thank you." When you next express thanks to God or to another person, make it heartfelt and personal.

God's Word

Shout for joy to God,
all the lands!
Serve God with gladness!
Come into God's presence with joyful singing!
Know that Yahweh is God!
Yahweh made us, and we belong to God;
we are God's people and the sheep of God's pasture.

Enter God's gates with thanksgiving
and the courts with praise!
Give thanks to God; bless God's name!
For Yahweh is good;
God's steadfast love endures forever,
and God's faithfulness to all generations.

(Psalm 100)

Closing prayer: My God, I thank you for the gift of life today, for your creation, your life within me, and the people who have given me life. I am grateful for your gifts, past and present. I thank you in advance for your care of me and ask your grace to overcome any sufferings that I may encounter.

The Long Loneliness

Theme: Seeking God is the movement of the heart toward divine love. Dorothy describes this spiritual hunger, life without full union with God and the human community, as a long loneliness.

Opening prayer: "O God, you are my God whom I eagerly seek." (Psalm 63:1)

About Dorothy

Dorothy Day named her autobiographical book, published in 1952, *The Long Loneliness*. She said:

Tamar is partly responsible for the title of this book in that when I was beginning it she was writing me about how alone a mother of young children always is. I had also just heard from an elderly woman who had lived a long and full life, and she too spoke of her loneliness. I thought again, "The only answer in this life, to the loneliness we are all bound to feel, is community. The living together, working together, sharing together, loving God and loving our brother, and living close to him in community so we can show our love for Him." (P. 243)

Later in her life, Dorothy talked with Robert Coles about the same topic. Subsequently, Coles recounted their conversation:

> She longed for a meeting with someone, rather than anyone, and could not muffle the sound. She knew she would be lonely even when she acknowledged that cry, but she also recognized that she was not "alone," that her yearnings were ancient ones reaching back to Galilee, to the Garden, to the cry of cries, with the loudest possible echo over the centuries of time.
>
> Her loneliness, then, was existential, her restlessness the impatience and hunger of the voyager whose destination is far off. After we had sat together in silence, she added a last few words. "My conversion? My conversion was a way of saying to myself that I knew I was trying to go someplace and that I would spend the rest of my life trying to go there and try not to let myself get distracted by side trips, excursions that were not to the point." (Robert Coles, *Dorothy Day: A Radical Devotion*, p. 64)

Pause: Do you sometimes experience a similar long loneliness?

Dorothy's Words

Something happened to me when I was around twenty-five. I think I began to feel myself drifting toward nowhere. I had lived a full and active life, and I was glad I had met so many good people, interesting and intelligent people. But I yearned for something else than a life of parties and intense political discussions, though I still like to sit and discuss what is happening in the world: "current events" as they say in high school. When I fell in love with Forster I thought it was a solid love—the kind we had for a while—that I had been seeking. But I began to realize it wasn't the love between a man and a woman that I was hungry to find, even though I had enjoyed that love very much and Forster and I were as close as could be. When I became pregnant I thought it was a *child* I had been seeking, motherhood. But I realized that wasn't the answer either: I loved Forster, I was as happy as I had ever been when pregnant, and when Tamar was born I was almost delirious with joy, and I could hold and hold and hold her, and feel that with her in my arms my life's purpose had been accomplished.

But only for so long did I feel like that, I have to admit. No, it wasn't restlessness. . . . For years, when people talked with me about my youth, about my life in New York before I became a Catholic, they have always brought up the subject of my loneliness and my restlessness. I am to blame for the mention of loneliness, though I didn't mean the word as it has been taken by so many people. I meant a spiritual hunger; that's what I had in mind—a loneliness that was in me, no matter how happy I was and how fulfilled in my personal life. Once I was sitting and talking with Jacques Maritain. I told him that everyone wants to understand the mind, but no one is interested in understanding the soul. . . . He laughed, Maritain; he said it wasn't like that in the past, and it doesn't have to be, either. He said, "It doesn't have to be like that for you and me, if we take care." I was grateful for what he said, especially the expression "take care." . . .

. . . I have been asking *why* all my life; when you ask why, you're alone, because you don't ask answers from other people of questions that are not answerable— by other people. If you keep asking the question, you're restless, I suppose; but not restless in the psychological sense. You are wondering why we're here and what this time we're here means. You're restless spiritually. Lots of our visitors are struggling with the same religious and philosophical questions that Jacques Maritain put to himself, and of course, dear Peter. . . . [Peter] was lonely only in the sense that he missed being near to God all the time. But he had a vision of God, and so he wasn't really lonely at all. He was—I think it is true for many of us— lonely only because of what he *saw, saw ahead,* the moment of that meeting, that reconciliation between the human world and the divine one. Oh, I'm getting above my height here! (Coles, *A Radical Devotion,* pp. 61–63)

Reflection

Yearning for God, spiritual hunger, divine restlessness, the long loneliness are all phrases partially describing the mystery of the human heart seeking union with ultimate reality. No sole human, no possession, no power can fulfill, satisfy, or alleviate this yearning, hunger, and loneliness.

Only the Spirit of God can lead us home to God and to communion with the People of God: "We have all known the long loneliness and we have learned that the only solution is love and that love comes with community" (*Long Loneliness*, p. 286). Rather than being the source of desperation, the long loneliness—embraced—leads us to open our hearts, minds, and souls to God and to one another.

✧ We experience spiritual hunger or the long loneliness uniquely. In writing, or by using paints, clay, watercolors, or some other medium, try to depict spiritual hunger as it manifests itself in your life.

✧ In her twenties, Dorothy sat in a tavern and listened to the writer Eugene O'Neill, in a dour mood, recite from Francis Thompson's poem "The Hound of Heaven":

> I fled Him, down the nights and down the days;
> I fled Him, down the arches of the years;
> I fled Him, down the labyrinthine ways
> Of my own mind; and in the mist of tears
> I hid from Him, and under running laughter.
> Up vistaed hopes, I sped;
> And shot, precipitated,
> Adown Titanic glooms of chasmèd fears,
> From those strong Feet that followed, followed after.
> But with unhurrying chase
> And unperturbèd pace,
> Deliberate speed, majestic instancy,
> They beat—and a Voice beat
> More instant than the Feet—
> "All things betray thee, who betrayest me."

Meander through your neighborhood or a park and recite these verses as you go along. Or, just use one phrase from the poem as a prayer to repeat rhythmically.

✧ Who is your Peter Maurin, the person who most clearly manifests the benefits of a spiritual life for you? Write about your spiritual mentor's character, the events of his or her life, the gifts she or he shows you. Write a letter (to send or not) or a prayer of thanksgiving for your spiritual mentor.

✧ Read the story of the prodigal son in Luke 15 and imagine yourself in that story. Reflect on the loneliness of the son in the foreign country, the choice to return, and the father's welcome. Have you felt like a stranger in a strange land? Do you wish to return to your spiritual home? What sort of welcome do you expect to receive? Sing a song of rejoicing for the spiritual hunger that leads you back to God and to community.

✧ Use the quotation from the Song of Songs in God's Word and reflect on what, or whom, you are seeking in your life.

God's Word

> Each night in bed I yearned
> for the one that my heart loves.
> I cannot find my love!
> So I will desert my bed in the wee hours of morning
> and go through the city's streets
> to seek the one my heart longs for.
> But, my love was nowhere to be found.
> Longingly, I asked the sentinels,
> "Have you seen the one I love?"
>
> (Adapted from Song of Songs 3:1–3)

Closing prayer:

O God, you are my God whom I eagerly seek;
for you my flesh longs and my soul thirsts
like the earth, parched, lifeless, and without water.
I have gazed toward you in the sanctuary
to see your power and your glory.
For your love is better than life;
my lips shall glorify you.

(Psalm 63:1–3)

✧　**Meditation 15**　✧

Becoming Community

Theme: Our love of God and neighbor are drawn together by living in common with other people.

Opening prayer: God, you constantly call us to be a people united in your love. Give me brothers and sisters with whom I might live and share your life and love.

About Dorothy

After 1933, Dorothy went to bed most nights in a Catholic Worker House of Hospitality or at one of the movement's farms. During her travels around the country, she often stayed at Catholic Worker houses. She died at Maryhouse, in the New York City neighborhood where the movement began. The Catholic Worker was Dorothy's home and community.

Dorothy stayed in many buildings—on Fifteenth Street, Charles Street, Mott Street, Chrystie Street, Ludlow Street, at the Easton and Newburg farms, at the beach house on Staten Island, but the people and shared life inside the houses of hospitality formed her community. Those who came were a moveable feast of humanity.

Guests of every color, creed, and condition came for Catholic Worker hospitality: the burned-out and alcoholic professionals, the disease-ridden derelicts, the pregnant, single women, the immigrants, the unemployed, and those suffering mental anguish or illness; mostly people down on their luck, the abandoned people of an affluent society. These guests could be good-humored, quarrelsome, helpful, or a noisy pain in the neck. All were welcome, and some guests stayed on for the rest of their lives.

Throughout the years, many people also knocked at the Catholic Worker door to seek answers for their lives: young men and women with Christian ideals, people in midlife, uncertain of what God wanted them to do. Even some old friends of Dorothy's came, needing solace. Those who came were mostly lay Catholics, but many priests, sisters, seminarians, and people of other faiths came to experience the Catholic Worker community and to enliven their commitments:

> Characters of every description and from every corner of life turned up—and we welcomed them all. They "joined" The Catholic Worker in many ways. Some came with their suitcases, intending to stay with us a year, and, shocked by our poverty, lingered only for the night. Others came for the weekend and remained for years. (*Loaves and Fishes*, p. 35)

All who stayed a while were marked with new ideals and values when they left. Struggles, disagreements, and occasional bitterness dwelled with celebrations, enormous energy, and love. Stanley Vishnewski, who was a Catholic Worker with Dorothy for forty-five years, in his characteristic wit sometimes called the Catholic Worker "a house of hostility" (*Loaves and Fishes*, p. 38).

The daily life that Dorothy shared with guests and workers alike involved performing the works of mercy: serving meals, distributing clothing, conversing (there was always conversation), cleaning, and getting out *The Catholic Worker* newspaper. It was the life of a family house, a very large one. A daily rhythm of worship and prayer wove into this daily round of work. For Dorothy and many of the workers, each day began with early Mass at a nearby parish church and, if time allowed, a period for meditation or scripture reading. After the noon meal, a bell signaled the time to pray the rosary.

Those who wished and were able joined in some part of the Divine Office or evening prayers before bed.

Dorothy reflected about the Catholic Worker community: "Ah, those early days that everyone likes to think of now since we have grown so much bigger; that early zeal, that early romance, that early companionableness! . . . It is a permanent revolution, this Catholic Worker Movement." (*Long Loneliness*, p. 186)

Pause: Ponder this question: What is your community?

Dorothy's Words

We were just sitting there talking when Peter Maurin came in.

We were just sitting there talking when lines of people began to form, saying, "We need bread." We could not say, "Go, be thou filled." If there were six small loaves and a few fishes, we had to divide them. There was always bread.

We were just sitting there talking and people moved in on us. Let those who can take it, take it. Some moved out and that made room for more. And somehow the walls expanded.

We were just sitting there talking and someone said, "Let's all go live on a farm."

It was as casual as all that, I often think. It just came about. It just happened.

I found myself, a barren woman, the joyful mother of children. It is not easy always to be joyful, to keep in mind the duty of delight.

The most significant thing about *The Catholic Worker* is poverty, some say.

The most significant thing is community, others say. We are not alone any more.

But the final word is love. At times it has been, in the words of Father Zossima, a harsh and dreadful thing, and our very faith in love has been tried through fire.

We cannot love God unless we love each other, and to love we must know each other. We know Him in the breaking of bread, and we know each other in the breaking of bread, and we are not alone any more. Heaven is a banquet and life is a banquet, too, even with a crust, where there is companionship.

We have all known the long loneliness and we have learned that the only solution is love and that love comes with community.

It all happened while we sat there talking, and it is still going on. ("Postscript," *Long Loneliness*, pp. 285–286)

Reflection

The word *community* is used so often today and in so many contexts that it might be difficult to appreciate what community meant to Dorothy. Community is applied to all kinds of groups, from the people of the whole planet to a small circle of friends. More often than not, the word is applied in a wishful sense. We yearn for community and want our groupings to be a community. At the same time, we know that our associations are often shallow, and we remain isolated and alone in spite of the words we use.

Dorothy's notion of community implied people joined together to live as radical Christians. Jesus' commandment to love one another and to strive to fulfill the Sermon on the Mount and the challenge of Matthew 25 provided the foundation for life together. She sought no mandate or direct support for God's work from the state or ecclesiastical authorities. In the process of community life, Dorothy envisioned that both those who came to a Catholic Worker community and the whole society would be transformed by Christ's love.

Coexisting with her idealism about community was Dorothy's realism. Once Dorothy tried to dissuade a woman who made a generous offer of money and wanted to come live with the community:

I tried to discourage her by describing, in detail, the kind of people we were, the kind of people she would have to live with. I explained that we were not a community of saints but a rather slipshod group of individuals who were trying to work out certain principles—the chief of which was an analysis of man's freedom and what it implied" (*Loaves and Fishes*, p. 47).

Community required effort, openness, and lots of talk.

The postscript to *The Long Loneliness* in Dorothy's Words serves as a prescription and rule for the kind of community Dorothy envisioned. Based on love, shown in the works of mercy, Catholic Workers come together in reality and in the breaking of the bread. It is an invitation to be at home as Dorothy was:

> The only answer to this life, to the loneliness we are all bound to feel, is community. The living together, working together, sharing together, loving God and loving our brother, and living close to him in community so we can show our love for Him. (*Long Loneliness*, p. 243)

✧ On a sheet of paper, list the qualities of community life that Dorothy describes in her postscript to *The Long Loneliness*. Then list the *communities* in which you have lived and participated: for example, your family, school, seminary or religious congregation, your neighborhood and parish, and so on. Where have you been most at home and able to experience the love of brothers and sisters in Christ? Offer a prayer of thanksgiving for times of joy and grace in community. Ask God to give you a forgiving heart for times of trial and suffering in community. Finally, ask God to give you a community of healing, grace, joy, faith and, above all, love.

✧ Slowly read God's Word, which is taken from the Acts of the Apostles, and dwell on the Christian life lived then. Then reread Dorothy's Words again, dwelling on the Christian life she describes. Choose a word or phrase that strikes you and repeat it silently as a prayer. Let the words challenge and inspire you.

✧ Dorothy once called the Catholic Worker Movement "a freelance movement," one that lacked formal structure, rules, and predictability. It formed because the people were open and responsive to God's call. Let your imagination open itself to God's call to be compassionate, to love totally, and to create community. Remove your assumptions and the boundaries of your present life from your imagination. Is there a summons to expand your community? Do you hear an invitation?

✧ Community life for Dorothy involved a rhythm that combined three elements: the everyday life of a family, the practice of the works of mercy, and the rhythm of worship and prayer. Is that rhythm present in your life? Is one or another element missing or exaggerated? How might you establish or restore the rhythm of Christian community?

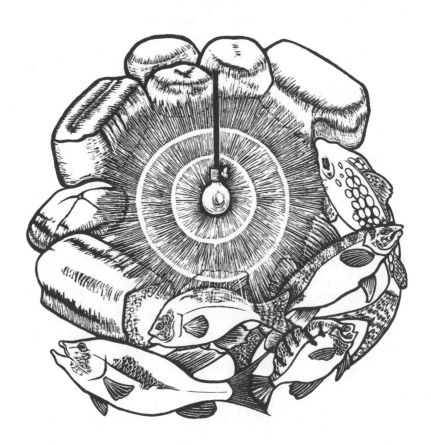

God's Word

These remained faithful to the teaching of the apostles, to the [community], to the breaking of the bread and to the prayers.

And everyone was filled with awe; the apostles worked many signs and miracles.

And all who shared the faith owned everything in common; they sold their goods and possessions and distributed the proceeds among themselves according to what each one needed.

Each day, with one heart, they regularly went to the Temple but met in their houses for the breaking of the bread; they shared their food gladly and generously; they praised God and were looked up to by everyone. (Acts 2:42–47)

Closing prayer:

God . . .
all-powerful, Christ . . . Savior, Spirit of love.
You reveal yourself in the depths of our being,
drawing us to share in your life and your love.
One God, three Persons,
be near to the people formed in your image,
close to the world your love brings to life.

("Opening Prayer," Liturgy for Trinity Sunday,
The Roman Missal)

F·R·E·E·D·O·M

✧ For Further Reading ✧

Selected Books by Dorothy Day

By Little and By Little: The Selected Writings of Dorothy Day. Robert Ellsberg, ed. New York: Alfred A. Knopf, 1983. Also reissued as *Dorothy Day: Selected Writings.* Robert Ellsberg, ed. Maryknoll, NY: Orbis, 1992.

From Union Square to Rome. Silver Spring, MD: Preservation of Faith Press, 1938.

House of Hospitality. New York: Sheed & Ward, 1939.

Loaves and Fishes. New York: Harper & Row, 1963.

The Long Loneliness: The Autobiography of Dorothy Day. New York: Harper & Row, 1952.

On Pilgrimage. New York: Catholic Worker Books, 1948.

On Pilgrimage: The Sixties. New York: Curtis Books, 1972.

Therese. Springfield, IL: Templegate Publishers, 1960.

Selected Books about Dorothy Day and the Catholic Worker Movement

Coles, Robert. *Dorothy Day: A Radical Devotion.* Reading, MA: Addison-Wesley Publishing Company, 1987.

Coy, Patrick G., ed. *A Revolution of the Heart: Essays on the Catholic Worker.* Philadelphia: New Society Publishers, 1988.

Egan, Eileen. *Dorothy Day and the Permanent Revolution.* Erie, PA: Pax Christi USA, 1983.

Forest, Jim. *Love Is the Measure: A Biography of Dorothy Day.* New York: Paulist Press, 1986; Maryknoll, NY: Orbis, 1994.

Merriman, Brigid O'Shea. *Searching for Christ: The Spirituality of Dorothy Day*. South Bend, IN: University of Notre Dame, 1994.

Miller, William D. *Dorothy Day: A Biography*. San Francisco: Harper & Row, 1982.

Troester, Rosalie Riegle, comp. and ed. *Voices from the Catholic Worker*. Philadelphia: Temple University Press, 1988.

Acknowledgments *(continued)*

The excerpts on pages 41–42 and 52 are from *Voices from the Catholic Worker,* compiled and edited by Rosalie Riegle Troester (Philadelphia: Temple University Press, 1988), pages 62 and 79, respectively. Copyright © 1988 by Temple University. Used by permission of Temple University Press.

The following are from articles by Dorothy Day as published in *The Catholic Worker* newspaper. The excerpt on page 42 is from "The Mystical Body of Christ" (October 1939). The excerpt on pages 46–47 is from "A Room for Christ" (December 1945). The excerpt on page 68 is from "On Pilgrimage" (May 1948). The excerpt on pages 75–76 is from "Poverty and Precarity" (May 1952). The excerpt on pages 99–101 is from "Our Country Passes from Undeclared to Declared War; We Continue Our Christian Pacifist Stand" (January 1942). The excerpts on pages 28, 68–69, 69 (second excerpt), 76, 82–83, 94, 94–95, and 106–107 are from various articles by Dorothy Day as published in *The Catholic Worker* newspaper. Used with permission.

The excerpts on page 46 (first and second excerpt), 73, and 90 (second excerpt) are from *House of Hospitality,* by Dorothy Day (New York: Sheed & Ward, 1939), pages 44, 43, 69, and 64, respectively. Copyright © 1939 by Sheed & Ward.

The following are from articles by Dorothy Day as published in *The Commonweal*. The excerpt on page 59 is from "The Scandal of the Works of Mercy" (4 November 1949). The excerpt on page 63 is from "Traveling by Bus" (10 March 1950), page 577. Used by permission of Commonweal.

The extract on pages 63–64 is from *On Pilgrimage: The Sixties,* by Dorothy Day (New York: Curtis Books, 1972), pages 281–282. Copyright © 1972 by Tamar Hennessy. Permission applied for.

The excerpt on pages 67–68 is from *On Pilgrimage,* by Dorothy Day (New York: Catholic Worker Books, 1948), pages 174–175.

The excerpts on page 72 (second excerpt) and 123 are from *The Roman Missal.* Copyright © 1973 by the International Committee on English in the Liturgy (ICEL). The excerpt on pages 103–104 is from the English translation of *Eucharistic Prayers for Masses of Reconciliation.* Copyright © 1975, ICEL. Used with permission. All rights reserved.

Titles in the Companions for the Journey Series

Order from your local religious bookstore or from

Saint Mary's Press
702 TERRACE HEIGHTS
WINONA MN 55987-1320
USA
1-800-533-8095